MADE
FOR THIS

40 DAYS TO LIVING YOUR PURPOSE

JENNIE ALLEN

W Publishing Group

AN IMPRINT OF THOMAS NELSON

Published in Nashville, Tennessee, by W Publishing Group, an imprint of Thomas Nelson.

Published in association with Yates & Yates, LLP, www.yates2.com.

Thomas Nelson titles may be purchased in bulk for educational, business, fund-raising, or sales promotional use. For information, please e-mail SpecialMarkets@ThomasNelson.com.

Unless otherwise noted, Scripture quotations are taken from the Holy Bible, New International Version®, NIV®. © 1973, 1978, 1984, 2011 by Biblica, Inc.™ Used by permission of Zondervan. All rights reserved worldwide.

Scripture quotations marked ESV are from the ESV® Bible (The Holy Bible, English Standard Version®), © 2001 by Crossway, a publishing ministry of Good News Publishers. Used by permission. All rights reserved.

Scripture quotations marked GNT are from the Good News Translation in Today's English Version—Second Edition. Copyright 1992 by American Bible Society. Used by permission.

Scripture quotations marked KJV are from the King James Version.

Scripture quotations marked NLT are from the *Holy Bible*, New Living Translation. © 1996, 2004, 2007, 2013 by Tyndale House Foundation. Used by permission of Tyndale House Publishers, Inc., Carol Stream, Illinois 60188. All rights reserved.

Any Internet addresses, phone numbers, or company or product information printed in this book are offered as a resource and are not intended in any way to be or to imply an endorsement by Thomas Nelson, nor does Thomas Nelson vouch for the existence, content, or services of these sites, phone numbers, companies, or products beyond the life of this book.

ISBN 978-0-7852-2909-4 (eBook)

Library of Congress Control Number: 2018914418

ISBN 978-0-7852-2907-0 (HC)

Printed in the United States of America

21 22 23 24 LSC 6

Dedicated to four of the greatest dreams God had for my life:
Conner, Kate, Caroline, and Cooper Allen.
You are my favorites.

CONTENTS

PART 3: THE THREADS

PART 4: THE FUTURE

MADE FOR THIS

I am not really good at anything."

The tears came first and then a slew of words that felt like lies. Really, they *were* lies, but the person saying the words obviously believed she was telling the truth.

"I don't know if I have ever done anything truly important."

"I feel like I have missed my purpose."

"I don't know what to do next."

Sarah was a couple of years from an empty nest. What were once quiet, pesky thoughts now grew louder. She didn't look directly at me; her eyes darted around as if they might land somewhere more comfortable. But they couldn't find their home.

Her son, Isaiah, had popped in during our short coffee break. He had a firm handshake and told me he was almost eighteen. I noticed his shirt was ironed and tucked in because I have a son the same age who also tucks in his ironed shirt. He does this because I don't iron them, so he learned how to do it.

All I wanted to do was wrap Sarah up and get her away from whoever was making her believe these lies! But I knew that the person was her.

"Sarah, are you a good mom?" I had already met her son with an ironed shirt, and I knew. Like I knew she had a dozen or more superpowers that she couldn't see. I knew because God built her and set her in this time and promised to equip her with gifts and a purpose. I just knew.

Her eyes finally met mine. She grinned through her tears and said, "I am a great mom. That is the one thing I can do, but that is about to be over."

————

So what is our purpose on earth? Why are we here?

Though that conversation happened exactly two hours ago, I meet a Sarah, and sometimes ten Sarahs, every single day.

Sometimes she's a twenty-four-year-old dating a man who does not know Jesus. He barely values anyone but himself, but she can't bring herself to break up with him because she's afraid no one else will come.

Sometimes she is sixty-two and has both margin to make disciples and a passion for it, but she is divorced and can't see what she has to offer younger women in her church. So, rather than invest in their lives, she withdraws and disqualifies herself.

Sometimes she is sixteen and can't figure out how to quit obsessing about herself. She keeps thinking about her weight, stepping on a scale, and scrolling Instagram. She wants to please Jesus, and love people, but she doesn't know how to turn off the loud voices in her head telling her she cannot ever measure up.

Sometimes we tell ourselves the lies, and sometimes someone else has lied to us. Either way, these lies are from the Enemy, who is out to shut down the church.

But I have also seen the opposite. I have seen women believe God. Women who have been set free, who believe the truth about God and themselves and their purpose here. They are nonchalantly—almost without thinking—radically laying down their gifts and resources to display Jesus and meet the needs around them. And it's dangerous to hell.

So why *are* we here?

Since the release of my books *Anything* and *Restless*, I've watched women come alive. They're finding that they were made for great purposes that can change eternity in the hearts and lives of others. I've heard their stories and seen them transformed through the prayer of surrender and intentional discovery of the great adventure God has written for them.

I want the same for you.

Acts 17:26–27 says, "[God] marked out their appointed times in history and the boundaries of their lands. God did this so that they would seek him and perhaps reach out for him and find him."

So let's go on a journey together. Forty days to be exact. Forty days to remember how delightful Jesus is, to be reminded of who you are, to consider that you are a part of the story of God with a part to play in it. It's forty days to hope hopes and dream dreams and pray prayers. Forty days to become dangerous to the Enemy again, or maybe for the first time.

Join us, will you?

This forty-day approach is a new look at the core message of my first two books *Anything* and *Restless*. We've combined them to create a unique, interactive journey to help you analyze the places you find yourself in, your passions, your gifts, your experiences, your age, and your positions to discover your specific calling. Then we've provided the space to work it out. You'll also find a few stories along the way to show how other women have moved beyond fear, uncertainty, and excuses to find what they were made for.

But before we dig in to learning about our purpose and calling, let's recognize we all already have one: "to make disciples of all nations" (Matt. 28:19). In that we are the same. It's how we live it out that is unique.

Let's do this together!

We are a team on a mission, and we need you to jump in with all of yourself: everything you have and everything you are, fighting the lies, being dangerous to the Enemy. Come on! You were made for this.

PART 1

THE PRAYER

PRAYING *ANYTHING*

*We are God's handiwork, created in Christ Jesus to do good
works, which God prepared in advance for us to do.*

—EPHESIANS 2:10

God, we will do anything. *Anything.*"

That night as I was falling asleep, after my husband Zac and I prayed *anything*, I looked up at God and asked Him, *What do You want me to do while I'm here?*

We were just so tired of normal. We loved our simple, sane life, but now we wanted to find the kind of life you only find if you lose normal, simple, and sane. God was real and heaven was coming, and I wanted to hold every moment on earth in light of when I would meet God face-to-face. We didn't want to hold on to life as we knew it. There was something bigger than us and our little story playing out on this spinning planet, and we wanted in.

ALL IN

This is a journey that starts with deciding you're all in. That you're made for something more, and you're over living for anything less. You're over living a cute, comfortable, easy life. Sick of making decisions based on your own limited adequacy and capacity because, if God is real and who He says He is, why would you?

If you're like me when I prayed *anything*, you don't want to waste your life. I didn't want to miss what God had for me because I was afraid to let go of what I knew. I was ready to forsake this life for the next. I wanted Him to unreservedly have me, so that when I faced Him, we would both know that my life was spent on everything He had dreamed for me. I wanted to be right with God at the end of my life rather than right with all the people in it.

To get to that point, I had to be ruined for ordinary life. Reading the blog of a girl named Katie Davis Majors, who had given up a comfortable life to adopt thirteen kids in Uganda—all because she was in love with Jesus—I grieved.[1] I grieved the life I had built around a plastic god and a pretend heaven. I grieved a life that was spent on myself, the excess I had justified while others suffered. I grieved sitting back and controlling my image rather than pouring out my life and gifts for the kingdom of God. I grieved that my mind had been spent solving my own simple problems rather than giving my life away.

Why had I sat on every gift God had given me to make Him known? Because I cared more about being judged by everyone else but Him?

It devastated me because I almost got away with a wasted life. But it was like God lifted my head and let me see into His heart, into heaven, into the brokenness of those suffering, into my own soul. And in a moment what had never occurred to me made perfect sense. So much sense that I was willing . . . desperately willing . . . to do *anything*.

SOMETHING BIGGER

Honestly, I think most people are craving something bigger than comfort and an easy life. I think, if you are starting this journey, you are someone who feels that too. We were made for this bigger story . . . we were made to show the glory of God and to fight dark cosmic forces, even in parts of life that seem mundane. I know—it still sounds insane to me too. But it's real, and it's our story. And we were made for this. Now we discover what part we play in it by being wholly consecrated to Him. By praying *anything*.

Henry Varley said, "The world has yet to see what God will do with a man fully consecrated to him."[2] I don't know if the world has seen it yet, but I do think we've found ourselves in the midst of a generation who would like to try. I want to try.

This is a journey toward living in that bigger story God has for you. Toward leaping, fighting, wrestling, and searching until you lay hold of it. Take these forty days to go deep—to search your restless soul, to dig through Scripture, and to know the heart of God so as to find your place in it. While at times it will be hard, at times exhilarating, at times beautiful and even terrifying, it will be worth it. Even if it is overwhelming and costly, it will be worth it because God is worth it.

AGAINST THE CURRENT

I look around and see currents that have dug deep crevices in our culture and eventually carved them into our souls. Currents that make us think:

- These seventy to eighty years of life feel long and important.
- Comfort and safety are worthy pursuits.
- Stuff matters.
- Happiness is my right as an American.
- Moral living pleases God.

As a generation, I believe we are all yawning and waking up, identifying these currents, and comparing them to the truth of God. We're considering this simple but game-changing thought: *If God is really real and we are going to live with Him forever, shouldn't He be the only thing? Shouldn't He be the controlling force of our lives? If we really believe this?*

We feel a growing desire not to become like the religious people God referred to when He said, "This people draw near with their mouth and honor me with their lips, while their hearts are far from me" (Isa. 29:13 ESV).

And everyone is asking the question, *Do I believe in the invisible enough that I'm willing to live for it?*

It is a call to childlike faith. The simple reaction a child has to truth is to believe, act, and live as if truth is true. Simply. Recklessly. Christ said: "Truly, I say to you, unless you turn and become like children, you will never enter the kingdom of heaven" (Matt. 18:3 ESV). *Anything* is a prayer of childlike trust—trust that no matter what He asks you to do, He will do something beautiful with you. No matter how unprepared, inept, or ordinary you might feel, He's holding your hand

If you look at every significant impact for God's kingdom—from Paul in Acts to D. L. Moody to Billy Graham to Mother Teresa—these were all average people, sometimes the least likely people, who were just completely resigned to God.

Zac and I, we wanted in on this. We wanted to know what works God had prepared in advance for us to do. We wanted into the stories that last forever. We wanted to quit being swept along with the current and building lives that did not matter for eternity. We wanted to not just offer God words but truly offer up our lives and all that was in them, letting go of every expectation of what He would say.

"God, we will do anything. *Anything*." Our lives now lay in the hands of a reckless, invisible God.

RESPOND

Write your own definition of *surrender*. What is it?

What does surrender cost?

What is the outcome of surrender for you?

In what ways, if any, are you sick of "normal"?

Think about wanting to be right with God at the end of your life rather than right with all the people in it. Can you discern between these two right now? What are the differences?

What do you need to let go of to offer your life and all that is in it to the Lord?

Here at the beginning, what do you hope to gain from this journey? Why do you think God has brought you to this point?

READ & REFLECT

What will your story be? In what will feel like only a minute, if you know Jesus as your Savior, we will be together in heaven. I am so excited that you are starting this journey toward living the story He has for you, and I cannot wait to meet face-to-face and hear it all. You better not bring me the safe version of a life! Bring the crazy stuff. Bring the unexplainable. Bring the story only God could write. I can't wait.

Read Acts 17:26 and Ephesians 2:10.

Acts says that God sets us in the generation and place we live. And in Ephesians Paul writes that before time, God planned the good works we would do. There are stories already written that we are to live. Are we living them?

After reading these passages, consider the answers to these two questions:

Who are You, Lord?
What do You want for me?

WHAT IS YOUR ANYTHING?

Whatever were gains to me I now consider loss for the sake of Christ.

—PHILIPPIANS 3:7

That night we prayed *anything,* I told God, "From this point on things are changing. I am living for the moment when I will face You. I want to get to heaven out of breath, having willingly done anything that You— God of the universe—asked me to do . . . anything."

Zac and I prayed *anything* every night for a week. Every night we offered up something else to God as though we were little kids; we lifted up our house to Him as if it were a little red plastic Monopoly house that we were willing to trade Him. We offered our home, our jobs, our places, and our talents, and step by step He answered yes or no, this way or that. Eventually He led us into radical, life-upending changes including adoption, new ministries, new cities, and other things beyond what we could have come up with by ourselves. But it started with the little everyday things. And as He peeled our grip off our lives, it hurt. As He asked us to jump, it terrified us. But we discovered that's how the best things start.

HOW TO PRAY *ANYTHING*

Praying *anything* is where it all begins. It's not just saying mere words or a reckless sacrifice; praying *anything* begins with love—actually loving a person. "If I give away all I have, and if I deliver up my body to be burned, but have not love, I gain nothing" (1 Cor. 13:3 ESV). Starting with love and moving through to obedience, here are the most important steps to praying the *anything* prayer.

1. *Experience Christ. Anything* begins with a relationship with the God of the universe through Christ, who says, "I am the way, and the truth, and the life. No one comes to the Father except through me" (John 14:6 ESV).

   Laying down all that we love more than Him is next, and that may take a while. It took many years of God chipping away at me, and even still it is a daily surrender. But after that—after you are all surrendered, willing, abandoned, sold out, and all in—then what?

2. *Pray.* Our story began long before we prayed. The night we uttered the words was just a step in the process of surrender. But it was an important step. God wants to be invited in to lead your life, for your heart to stand before Him and say, "You have me. Do anything with me." That is a bold, beautiful move. Continuing to mean it daily as His will unfolds will prove even more powerful. Ask Him to show you where He wants you to pour out your life and gifts and resources.

3. *God Speaks.* He speaks first through His Word. If I hadn't read God's Word to us about caring for the poor and the orphaned dozens of times, I would have never sensed His Spirit leading me to adopt. Or if it wasn't clear to me the passionate way Christ loved me and poured His life out for me, I would not be compelled to do the same

for others. We know who God is because of His Word; we must read it. His Spirit's leading always is tied up in His Word. We are to walk with God "in spirit and truth" (John 4:24 ESV). One without the other is not of God; it is either a false spirit or dead religion.

So you read and study and search and pray. Then you ask God to lead you. When we were feeling led in specific *anythings*, it wasn't through an audible voice. It was through promptings in our spirits, that burning in our gut when we know something is real. It burns, but it is also subtle, gentle, and mysteriously quiet. Sometimes He quickly makes himself clear, and sometimes it involves months of processing and wrestling with God till we know for sure. But He does still speak to our hearts because He has things for us here—things we cannot accomplish without Him.

4. *Band Together.* Surround yourself with people on the same mission. We were built to need people. We cannot passionately surrender and follow God alone. We were built for bands of brothers (and sisters) to fight beside us. Find a church, start a study or small group, get creative, but find people to live on a mission with who will make you better, help you remember, and help you live your *anythings*. Intentionally pursue people who make you better.

5. *Obey.* Do what He says—whatever He says. You will be miserable until you obey. Even if it is hard, even if it is costly, it will be worth it. No matter the cost . . . obey and trust Him with the consequences of that obedience. Whatever we considered valuable, it will pale in comparison to Him. These things, Paul said, "I consider them garbage, that I may gain Christ and be found in him" (Phil. 3:8). That's how they compare. He is more than worth giving whatever we have to give. Then He gets in and actually restores us, unwinds our mess of a head and soul. His mercy trumps the most epic of stories. This God is real, and He is worth my surrender.

> your kingdom come,
> your will be done,
>   on earth as it is in heaven. (Matt. 6:10)

When we have our lives in gripped hands and we consider handing them over, most of us get that feeling—fear mixed with adrenaline mixed with nausea. It feels as though we might die if we jump. But when I prayed *anything*, what I feared would bind me set me free. It stung like death, and it still feels like death, but that feeling is the key turning in the lock. On the other side of the pain is freedom, peace, joy, hope, and the loss of control. It's how we were made to live.

FALL

So why do it? Why pray *anything*—and then *do* anything?

What if these little acts of obedience were a small part of a matrix of dominoes unfolding the glory of God (small because, after all, I am a small domino in a huge matrix)? Could He bypass me and find another route? Of course—He is God.

But what if I laid down my life, my domino, and through that unleashed an army of others who laid down and unleashed their obedience? What if, through this matrix, God's glory was displayed?

Many dominoes have fallen behind me to allow me to fall. Watching friends fall into adoption prepared our hearts for falling into adoption. And countless mentors and friends have fallen into my life to help me to fall into ministry through writing.

We are all dominoes . . . we all have our place. What is yours?

I beg you—all of us—to fall. Fall into obedience that will shape the glory of God in our generation. We don't want to get to heaven and realize we missed it, that God rerouted around us.

Besides, I have a feeling that what God has for us are the best things in life. I don't want to miss them.

RESPOND

Why would you pray *anything*? Is God worth it to you?

When you think about what your *anything* is, where do you feel your heart taking you? What scares you most and makes you most excited? List these things and pray through them in reflection.

When you think about praying your own *anything*, what is the most difficult thing to release control of to God, to lift up to Him?

There is a temptation to think surrender should look like the radical, crazy stuff everyone can see. What small, quiet, obedient step is God calling you to right now?

If God actually told you what He wanted you to do, would you be afraid to do it? How do you imagine this will work itself out in your everyday and ordinary moments?

We have no idea how our small acts of obedience impact others. Some of our *anythings* feel flashy and fancy, but most fall in secret places. And that throws us. We think we need to do something grand to prove our surrender. But God is so pleased with the times of prayer and obedience that happen in secret. "Your Father who sees in secret will reward you" (Matt. 6:4).

Whose faith has most shaped yours? What is it about their obedience that has influenced you?

Get an hour alone and journal. Can you pray *anything*?
Do it. Today. Don't wait.
Write it out. Tear it out and share it with the people closest to you.
Take a photo and mark this decision. It's your turning point.

READ & REFLECT

Friends, we are getting in deep. I know I never promised you easy, but when it comes to actually praying this prayer, actually handing it all over, I have received many, many letters about how finally letting go has often been agonizing. It is.

Paul is one of my favorite models of surrender in Scripture. He describes the tensions so clearly and yet is so sure of his own surrender. His faith emboldens mine.

Read Philippians 3:7–11.

> What did Paul hold as his greatest possession?
> How did that affect his view of suffering?
> How did that affect his view of blessings?

After reading these passages, consider the answers to these two questions:

> Who are You, Lord?
> What do You want for me?

DAY 3

OUT OF CONTROL

What we preach is not ourselves, but Jesus Christ as Lord, and ourselves as your servants for Jesus' sake. For God, who said, "Let light shine out of darkness," made his light shine in our hearts to give us the light of the knowledge of God's glory displayed in the face of Christ.

—2 CORINTHIANS 4:5–6

Somewhere I picked up the idea that if things did not feel right or fall perfectly into place, God was not in them. I thought obeying God should feel pretty easy and convenient. For instance, if God was calling you to Rwanda, then He would have a buyer for your house in two weeks; and if not, then He likely wasn't in it. Okay, maybe not that extreme, but if obeying seemed too uncomfortable, I likely would have decided that it wasn't from God. Where did I get that?

In Scripture God promises we will have trouble in this world. Christ says, "If you are for Me, then the world will be against you. If you are not willing to lose everything you have, including your life, don't even follow Me. Expect persecution, and consider that a privilege" (Matt. 12:30; Luke 14:26; and Matt. 5:10, paraphrased).

All my life I thought I had God's stamp of approval because my life wasn't going badly. Suddenly I was faced with the fear that it might actually be the opposite. What if my life was going so beautifully because I wasn't chasing after God?

Even though the thousand problems in my soul had shifted toward one goal and one hope and I felt free, I had a new problem: life was getting hard, the pace was picking up, and I felt reluctant. As I began this journey I wrote:

May 5, 2009

What if He actually told me what it is He wants me to do . . . and I don't want to do it? We are in a vulnerable spot. We have told Him we will do anything.

Go. Stay. Speak. Be quiet. Stand up. Sit down. Redeem children. Redeem dirty dishes. Something big. Something small. Anything drastic. Nothing fancy. Anything.

I want to know Christ . . .

Yes!

And the power of His resurrection . . .

Yes!

And the fellowship of sharing in His suffering . . .

Um . . . maybe?

Becoming like Him in His death . . .

Not at all! Could I have Starbucks while I decide?

And somehow to attain to the resurrection of the dead . . .

Big yes!

Please, somehow, God save me! Some days I am willing and some days I feel reluctant. Maybe I could do whatever big or small things if He would help me . . .

God, overcome me. Please.

LINDSEY'S STORY

Lindsey and her husband, Chris, were in their comfort zone. They were teaching and coaching at a private Christian school they loved, and their kids were settled in and thriving. The arrival of a precious new baby made finances tight, but they committed to doing what it took to stay where they were and keep their kids enrolled in their school.

Then Lindsey prayed the *anything* prayer and started feeling restless for something bigger. She felt overwhelmed with the sense that God had more in store for them. "We felt God was stirring our hearts to move us forward to something new," she wrote to me, "but we just didn't know yet." Then circumstances overcame them. At a time when they felt they had no choices financially, they were both offered jobs at a public school that looked nothing like what they dreamed of.

"It was such a hard decision to leave," she said. "We always thought the only way the Lord would move us was through His favor in getting us a job that was a 'step up.' But that is not the way it was panning out. God moved us through disappointment—the reality that we just financially could no longer sustain working there. So many tears were cried in wondering what God was doing, where He was in all this, and why He would move us from somewhere we loved and believed in to somewhere that was diffi-cult and completely absent of a Christ-centered community—even for our children, who had to move schools with us."

Fast-forward further into Lindsey's journey, when she began to feel the threads of her life and talents weaving into a bigger dream: working at the collegiate level. When a position finally opened at her ideal school, the Christian college where she and her husband had gone, she fought back crippling doubts, inadequacy, and insecurity to apply. She felt in no way qualified, but she held on for dear life to Paul's instructions to "fan into flame the gift of God, which is in you through the laying on of my hands. For the Spirit God gave us does not make us timid, but gives us power, love and self-discipline" (2 Tim. 1:6–7). Then, after rounds of interviews, she was selected as the new associate dean of the school.

"We came to find out," she wrote, "that I was most appealing to the college because I had seen both sides of education—Christian and public school. One thing we have learned through all this is that God orchestrates every season and experience in our lives according to His perfect plan—even when it doesn't always make sense." God moves through disappointment, she says. "Faith in the unseen and in the waiting, I've learned, is all part of this journey of life and sanctification. Now, here's to new adventures!"

HOLD ON AND SCREAM

Risk is terrifying. I had prayed the prayer of *anything* as though I were about to launch on the Superman ride at Six Flags, my eyes closed tight and fingernails digging in. I was so afraid.

I can just imagine God thinking something like, *Thanks a lot, Jennie. Great. You'll be used by Me, but no one else will ever want to be because you are making it look so terrifying!*

But on the other hand, maybe He was thinking, *I love that she realizes she is going to need Me for this.*

Yes, we are inadequate. On the edge of risk, you always feel it. But we aren't powered by ourselves. In taking the risk and praying *anything*, I was strapped in and couldn't get off. My heart raced and I thought I might throw up. Yet all I had to do was hold on and scream. The ride did the work. I just held on and screamed.

As I did, God showed up. We began to know Him. We began to

live out what one of my favorite seminary professors had told us about knowing God: *The only exercise that works 100 percent of the time to draw one close to the real God is risk.* To risk is to willingly place your life in the hand of an unseen God and an unknown future, then watch Him come through. He starts to get real when you live like that.

When he said that to our class in the lecture hall, we were all speechless. Knowing God, really knowing Him, was getting more complicated. But if He was real, if He was God, then certainly He was worth knowing—not just the facts but knowing what it was like to launch on this ride and have His hand alone holding us up.

Scripture describes a radical, reoriented life for those who trust Christ—one full of living for the invisible and the future. It's a life fully surrendered to an invisible God, whose agenda contradicts mine—a life very different from the safe, comfortable one I found myself creating.

Stepping out wholly dependent on God to come through, stepping away from what is secure and comfortable exposes the holes in our faith. And then when God comes through, it expands our faith. We see Him move in greater ways. When we risk and He shows up, we see Him differently than if we were standing safely looking on.

RESPOND

Recall a time when you were glad God trumped you in your life.

Describe an experience that helped you to realize that your life was completely out of your control.

Where is your faith currently being tested?

What precious thing might you have missed if you had been afraid to risk? Take a moment to give thanks for that, and ask God to empower you to continue living for things you can't see yet.

The question everyone asks themselves when looking over the cliff, before jumping into the unknown deep, is *what do I have to lose?* What are you most afraid of losing in this life? List them under each subject.

Comfort

Success

Approval

Acceptance

Other

All of this comes down to identity. Who are you apart from your things, your image, your people, and your plans? Are you secure alone with God? Freedom comes through letting go.

READ & REFLECT

This journey never stops being terrifying. It isn't the brave ones who pray this *anything* prayer; it's the ones who believe God. These days I hear a lot about bravery. But no matter how risky my faith has become, I've never once felt especially brave or courageous. The only thing that enables me to walk forward is having my eyes fixed on Jesus.

The opposite of fear is not bravery and courage—the opposite of fear is faith.

Read 2 Corinthians 4:1–18.

In his letter to the Corinthians, how did Paul's understanding of Christ and the gospel affect . . .

his view of himself?
the purpose of his life?
the way he suffers?

After reading these passages, consider the answers to these two questions:

Who are You, Lord?
What do You want for me?

ANYTHING FOR HIS GLORY

*Father, I want those you have given me to be with me where
I am, and to see my glory, the glory you have given me
because you loved me before the creation of the world.*

—JOHN 17:24

What do I want most?

For me, there are so many things. I want a few silly, shallow things: I need my car washed right now, and I would love a new iPhone (mine was recently dropped in the bath), a night out with my husband, or a night to catch up on TV. I want deeper things such as close friendships, to be someone my kids want to emulate, and for my words to make a difference. But what do I want most? What's the deepest desire of my soul? I cannot name it, but I am certain it centers entirely around me, a selfish desire to be important or appreciated, to "matter" or "be seen." Something like that.

What does God want most?

I've always known the answer, though I've never known what the answer meant. I certainly never knew what the answer meant for my life.

God is most after His glory.

Glory: it is a vague and mysterious word. John Piper defines God's glory as "the holiness of God put on display."[1] It's who God truly is, revealed so you can see and taste and feel Him, and in turn fall flat on your face.

JESUS PRAYED *ANYTHING*

When Jesus went to meet and plead with His Father before facing death, one word fell off His lips over and over again. He prayed for God's *glory*. He longed for it. He said He had spent his life on earth building and displaying it. Nothing mattered more to Him before His death than God showing Himself through Jesus and through us.

Even as I write these words today, I wonder if I honestly care. I can barely obey God without thinking, *What will it cost me?* I don't want to think that way. Left to myself, I am just that selfish. I want things. I want comfort and fun. I don't want to suffer. I want things to feel in control. Today I don't want to be typing and studying about God's glory—I'd rather be at Target or on Facebook.

What if we wanted what God wanted most? What if we wanted, like Jesus, God's glory above every other thing?

What if the true motive of my life and my heart were to make God known for a few years on this earth?

Jesus prayed this prayer: "Father, glorify Yourself through Me. Glorify Yourself through them" (John 17, paraphrased). Everyone sitting with Jesus that night felt the weight of that call, which was so large, so costly, so significant: the call to show the glory of God to the earth.

Jesus went on to pray, "I do not ask for these only, but also for those who will believe in me through their word . . . I am no longer in the world, but they are in the world" (John 17:20, 11 ESV). A few men meant to display God. Eventually, most of them were killed for this call. Friends, we're up. Those men are gone. Now we show God. We show His glory.

COMPELLED BY GLORY

We wake up every day to a world that needs us. All people everywhere are waking up and setting their feet on the earth, with their own responsibilities likely defined by whether their feet land on tile or wood or carpet or dirt.

But we all wake up and put our feet down every day, and we move through our time here according to the rules, expectations, demands, and hopes of our given space in this world. The given place in which I grew up issued a script that spelled out a life lived near family, in a safe neighborhood where you had a fence and cute curtains, and where life wasn't too hard, especially if you loved Jesus.

In John 17 Jesus prayed this for me and all of us who would come to know Him:

> You are not of this world, Jennie. You don't belong here. You are going to put your feet down every morning in this world, but you don't belong to it. You don't adhere to its rules and expectations. You don't even hope for the same things. Because you know Me and you are Mine, your home, your hope is with Me forever. Your expectations are that your short life here is spent on My mission even if it is costly. Because you know it is short.

If we pray *anything*, we will all, like Christ, be called to give up this life and things we love. We will be called to risk for His glory. Christ never intended for those who walked with Him to feel comfortable and safe. This was meant to be a risk-it-all pursuit. The glory of God will be made great on this earth, but what a privilege to be part of His plan to restore it.

Our God is compelling. He is asking us to go compel people to Him. To *compel* means to have a powerful or irresistible influence in the lives of others.

Many of us don't do this much. We avoid compelling anyone to God because it may feel cheesy or annoying. Well then, we have to find ways to compel that aren't cheesy or annoying. The problem with this new generation and their endearing disgust for "faking it" is that they run from church and organized religion. So we'll have to take God to them in a way that's real.

When my husband and I prayed *anything* with God's glory in mind, it all started to make sense. It all started to be real. Authenticity came without trying. What we once did in order to "matter" or to "be seen" we forgot all about. We matter and are seen because of God's love for us. Because there is an object to our actions, we move and love and restore, not so we matter but because we have been moved, loved, and restored by God.

Radical acts were not the goal; we were moved by a Person, in love with Christ. And out of that love came a willingness to trust and hand over our lives. Out of that, Jesus, because He is merciful, led us to the unique places where we would each give our lives away.

It spread in our church. Couples started praying *anything* with abandon. Hundreds of children were sponsored, friends relocated to impoverished neighborhoods to spread the gospel, families adopted and fostered. Others downsized their homes to give, reconciled with family members, forgave and pursued unity in our church, and let go of this life, longing to give themselves away in forgiveness and mercy because of Jesus. Because of His forgiveness and mercy. Because of His glory. Seeing it come to life is the highest goal of the *anything* prayer.

RESPOND

Do you struggle with forgetting about God as you go through your day-to-day life? What can you practically do to remember the supreme importance of God's glory each day?

Have you been burned by legalism? How can you avoid communicating legalism to your children, those you know, or loved ones who are growing in faith?

Why is God beautiful to you?

How do you think God might be calling you to start giving Him away rather than just learning about Him?

If you really believe that your life belongs to others as much as to yourself, how does that change your interactions with your family, community, and especially your church?

READ & REFLECT

No other passage shaped this project more than the verses you will be studying today. They recount the ultimate moment of surrender and perspective. Jesus is about to lay down His life for us. He is with His people, and He stops to pray for them. It is as if the heart of Jesus is laid bare before us. We see His thoughts, His goals, His passions, His hopes, and His plans.

Why would you pray *anything*? Is God worth it?

These verses scream yes to me. I pray you take significant time with these words and let them seep into your thoughts, your goals, your passions, your hopes, and your plans.

Read John 17:1–25.

How did Jesus view His Father?
What did He pray for us?
What did He believe could happen?

After reading these passages, consider the answers to these two questions:

Who are You, Lord?
What do You want for me?

STEPPING INTO HIS STORY

*In his great mercy he has given us new birth into a living hope
through the resurrection of Jesus Christ from the dead, and
into an inheritance that can never perish, spoil or fade.*

—1 PETER 1:3–4

P rayers like *anything* place us in the midst of stories. These stories have an
Author who writes characters, places, and parts. He develops story lines
that are actually quite epic, even if they feel momentarily insignificant.

In a million unique ways—as we change diapers, eat dinner, return
e-mails, pay the bills—we are to be the evidence of God. Jesus factored in
the mundane. We need to eat and sleep and shower and clean up and work
on our marriages because of the way He made us—typical, inadequate,
and human. Embrace the common: a Sunday afternoon watching sports,
coffee with a friend, cooking dinner for a neighbor, taking the dog for a
walk, heading to a job that is making you more humble and needy because
it is so unfulfilling, or working through conflict with a friend you have
offended. This and more is all part of it.

So do your everyday and your ordinary. Godliness is found and formed
in those places.

Jesus said the way we glorify God, the way we step into His story, is by accomplishing the work God gives us to do. While on earth Jesus glorified His Father by doing this very thing.

We play our part in His story, and the beauty is we were made for this.

We trust in God, who leads us to do spiritual things that may not totally make sense. God is still not very practical, and to follow Him takes trust. Following Him completely requires belief that He is good even if everything here and now is not, that He sees us and has an intentional plan for our few years here.

But before we can do anything, we need the Spirit to do anything, and He operates on a different level.

THE SPIRIT FUELS US

Until we believe in the reality of a spiritual war where spiritual beings exist and a spiritual plan is being accomplished, we won't need an invisible Spirit's help. It would seem ridiculous . . . unless it is all real.

I had made following Christ all about rules and principles. But the relationship I'd heard about growing up? This was it. God's Holy Spirit in me. Leaning into Him for self-control when my kids talk back, for guidance on where to use God's gifts in me, for words when I am writing, and for patience as the consequences of obeying flooded our lives.

Without the Spirit of God to lead our *anythings*, we will only be do-gooders with our own agendas. And they will fizzle. It will be a phase, some dramatic spiritual experiment we look back on fondly, wishing it had been real life. But sometimes the real thing takes time. We prayed *anything*, but it was over the course of months and years that our *anythings* have been revealed. I imagine this will continue for the rest of our lives; if we remain willing, more *anythings* are in store.

The Spirit is in us, those bound to Christ, and we wait on Him to act. We wait on Him to tell us what's next. This isn't easy, but it's pretty simple.

Service, or living your *anything*, is simply an expression of what is true about my God: He is trustworthy. I adore Him, so He has me . . . all of me. I don't choose my own path anymore. It is set for me, laid before the foundations of time. God prepared in advance the good works I would do (Eph. 2:10). That is the beautiful call on my life, on our lives. Led by the Spirit of God.

CALLED TO A PERSON

As our friends prayed and acted on their *anythings*, they weren't just recklessly saying yes to God's Spirit. They were also being set free from sin they had struggled with for years. As God got bigger, their thousand problems were shrinking. God was setting everyone free. Our affections, our goals, our futures had shifted. We were on a mission. Life was getting really fun because we were running with friends toward heaven, with abandon.

Abandonment only makes sense if there is a God worthy of abandoning everything for. The greatest gift in surrender is that in letting go of everything you think will fix you and make you feel better, you find a Person . . . not a pat answer or a verse or a cause. After your head clears from the struggle of wrestling yourself to the ground, you see a Person.

He was there before when you were preoccupied, but now you see Him.

Jesus said, "These things I have spoken to you, that my joy may be in you, and that your joy may be full" (John 15:11 ESV). And Scripture tells us, "We love because he first loved us" (1 John 4:19 ESV). He is our "living hope" (1 Peter 1:3).

When we don't love or feel joy or peace or passion, it's because we do not know His love or His joy or peace or passion. He is a Person, not a magic pill you take when your life or your soul is broken. He is a Person you talk to and listen to and love and respect. He's someone you decide to spend time with and dream with, someone you follow and learn from and hurt with—someone you choose over anybody else, over anything else. Jesus is a Person—*the* Person who defines my life, sweeps in, and changes me. When I let Him in.

We all want to be free, joyful, and peaceful, but we get reluctant to hand God everything. Yet that is part of the path to the things He promises us.

JUMP

At some point our faith and our words must become our actions and lives. But here is the beautiful, backward thing about risking everything for God: it is not the ones sitting out the dangerous parts who are finding life; it is the ones with everything at risk—heart racing, hopes high, purpose clear, and completely dependent and scared to death—who are really experiencing life.

The thing about following Jesus is He does things backward—freedom and true life came out of His death. In turn, to follow Christ to the cross, we jump: trusting Him with everything, praying *anything*, handing over every day and all that lives in it to a Person—in death we find life and freedom too.

God is often present right over the edges. Even so, "doing something," even something good, even something *great*, will never be the gospel. When we trust God with everything, He can explode our numb life into something beautifully meaningful.

We want God to knock out suffering and poverty. Ironically, He gave us just about all we need to do it. We give our lives to Him and He gives our lives away. Nothing on earth is more fun and more full than being distributed by an all-knowing, compassionate God, who knows exactly where our ridiculously blessed lives would be best spent.

There are a million creative ways to give our lives away, and we are going to find out what those are in the coming days. God is just waiting for us to jump.

RESPOND

In what area of your life is God asking not for radical sacrifice but simple obedience and your heart?

What agenda—maybe even a Christian agenda—do you need to set aside to follow Christ? Take a moment to sit with God and think of new ways you can get to know Him more as a person.

Read James 2:14–17. Do you talk more about God than you obey Him? In what area of your life are faith and words ready to become actions?

Over the past few days of this journey, you may have experienced a hint of the winds of change blowing. Looking over your answers to previous questions, what have you started to dream about how your life could be different in one or two years if you step out in that direction?

What are the first few steps you can take toward your anything? Consider sharing this with a small group, friend, or trusted mentor to support you as you grow.

READ & REFLECT

A day is coming when our eyes will close and there will be no more chaos. No one will be preaching or writing books about God to help us remember because we will be alive in that world with Him forever.

Anything is nothing in light of that. In light of forever. In light of Him—the Person. That day is coming faster than any of us realize. What will we do with the time we have been given? I want what Jesus wants for me, even if it costs me everything here.

Read 1 Peter 1:3–9.

> Based on this passage, what is promised?
> In light of that promise, how do you live from here?

After reading these passages, consider the answers to these two questions:

> Who are You, Lord?
> What do You want for me?

PART 2

THE CALL

DAY 6

RESTLESS

I will pour out my Spirit on all people.
Your sons and daughters will prophesy,
your young men will see visions,
your old men will dream dreams.

—ACTS 2:17

The most consistent question I have been asked by people who pray *anything* is some version of: "I am in. I am all surrendered to God. But now what? I don't know what He wants me to do." There's a sense of unease, of being on the precipice of something new, that I want us to dive into here. I feel this restlessness, too, and I know I'm not alone.

In the coming days we're going to examine and embrace this restless feeling and discover everything it means for us. It is the first whisper of the call on our lives—our purpose. The next nine days will be spent preparing our hearts to dream of what that call might be.

WHY DO WE FEEL THIS WAY?

I think we are all aching for some magical, great, noble purpose to squeeze into the holes of our ordinary lives. To know which direction to go in.

We are numb.

We are bored.

And yet, every once in a while our heart races just a little. Not like when we were kids and we heard the words *Disney World*. Not even as intensely as when we heard the ice-cream truck. But every once in a while it quickens.

Why such a restlessness for purpose?

Because *it is possible to waste our lives*.

These words haunt me and point to one of the greatest fears of mankind. We aren't sure we matter. We live with lots of things and lots of people, but do we live for something? We all desperately want to live for something greater than ourselves and our small pleasures. We die a little inside when we think we aren't, and we give up when we think we can't. But that purpose feels slippery sometimes. We glance over at people functioning in their gifts and God is using them in big ways, and we want that. But it can feel so far away.

There is a beautiful verse in the Bible hidden away in the book of Acts, describing the end of David's life: "When David had served God's purpose in his own generation, he fell asleep" (13:36).

King David was a man after God's heart who lived a passionate mess of a life, but he sought after God and God's will. God used him to change the history of the world. This verse has two truths that make me tremble:

1. God has a unique purpose for each of us in our generation.
2. We have the choice to live that purpose or not.

I want to serve the purpose of God in my generation before I fall asleep— before I die.

I am calling you to the same. If we, as a generation, serve the purposes of God on this earth, we could see our unwasted lives move together and change eternity. I want to attempt something in this journey together: *to dream*.

First, let's assume that if we are breathing, we have a specific purpose for being here. Every one of us with breath in our lungs still has something left to do.

I want to dream of what those purposes may be.

I wish I could promise magical moments with angels scripting visions in the sky just for you. I wish I could promise that at the end of this journey, you will never feel empty, numb, or bored again. I can't.

But if you go here with me, the drumbeat I hear in the distance—the one that makes my heart move faster—you will hear it. And maybe if we all hear and respond, we will see God move. We will know why we are here, why we are alive, what we are to do as a generation, and what we are to do as individuals.

So I am going to ask you to join me in an uncomfortable process during this journey. I want you to dare to believe that God has a vision for how you are to spend your life. Because finding and accomplishing this vision is quite possibly the greatest responsibility we have as a generation, second only to knowing and loving God.

WE WERE DESIGNED TO DREAM

God created man in His image for a purpose. In the beginning, in Genesis 1, only two jobs were ascribed to man:

1. Fill the earth with image bearers.
2. Make the world better: take chaos and give it order.

When we were born, we were given certain resources. Now we are to take whatever we were given and use it to reflect God and to serve people during our short time on earth. That's why we were given abilities above animals—to create, build, serve, lead, envision, and get after it. We have the unique talent of being able to see a need and then create a way to meet that need. In that way, we reflect God.

WE ARE CALLED TO DREAM

Through the prophet Joel, God said this of the future: "I will pour out my Spirit on all people. Your sons and daughters will prophesy, your old men will dream dreams, your young men will see visions" (Joel 2:28).

This day has happened. It's here.

You see, our creative God has an infinite number of creative plans to make Himself known through us in unique and beautiful ways.

The Spirit of God has dreams for you.

And He has given you an abundance of gifts, resources, people, and vision to accomplish *His* dreams for you. If you do not feel that way yet, you will.

What if?

What if the things you love to do aligned with the plans God has laid out for you from before the foundations of the earth?

What if the random relationships and activities in your life suddenly had focus and felt intentional and meaningful?

What if the things that caused you the most hurt became the birthplaces of your deepest passions?

What if you could get past your fears and insecurities and spend the rest of your life running your guts out after His purposes for you?

I still feel it sometimes . . . a whisper of more. Not more because what I am doing isn't important, but because I so rarely believe that it is.

May this journey be the place where your restless soul meets God, and where everyday moments become beautiful, and where no life or minute or breath ever feels small again.

RESPOND

Do you feel restless or discontent right now? If so, how does that discontentment tie into a desire for purpose?

Do you ever feel that what you are doing/ living is small or unimportant? What are those small things?

Do you believe God has a purpose for your life? What makes you feel that way?

When was the last time you dreamt about doing something specific in your life? What was it?

Are you coming into this study with any hurt and disappointment regarding your dreams? If so, describe it.

What do you hope to get out of the process of learning to dream again? What do you hope will change?

READ & REFLECT

The Holy Spirit flooded the earth at Pentecost. Immediately after, Peter reminded the apostles of the promise of that day.

Read Acts 2:14–21.

> What was that promise?
> Why was it given? (v. 21)

After reading these passages, consider the answers to these two questions:

> Who are You, Lord?
> What do You want for me?

PERMISSION TO DREAM

His divine power has given us everything we need for a godly life.

—2 PETER 1:3

The word *dream* used to contain some poetic magic when we were children. Dreaming possessed our minds. We dreamed that eggplants were really plants that make eggs, and being a policeman was the perfect profession because they shoot real guns, and fairies were interested in teeth and built castles with them somewhere. And we couldn't wait to fall in love and close our eyes and kiss a boy for the very first time at our wedding, which would have periwinkle-blue cupcakes and dresses and flowers.

God is a dreamer too. He built universes and generations of people out of His dreams. And God built us to dream.

> *dream (n.)*
> a visionary creation of the imagination . . .
> strongly desired goal or purpose.
> something that fully satisfies a wish.[1]

Dreaming strips life of its borders and sometimes of its reality and damage. Eventually we realize there are limits, and dreaming becomes something that only children do. Our imaginations evolve into problem-solving mechanisms. Because eventually enough of our dreams don't come true that we just stop bothering.

We were built with the ability to dream, but we've lost it.

What did you dream about as a kid?

What did you want to be when you grew up?

When did you stop dreaming?

I remember dreading adulthood. I dreamed about changing the world, purely and perfectly using my gifts, and it all felt possible. Most of us remember what it was like to live with whimsy, and nothing on earth felt out of our reach. If we could think of it, it was possible—no big deal.

We all used to be that way. But we have lost our whimsy. Our dreams have died, and in our pursuit of maturity, we have lost ourselves and even lost more of God.

MISSING GOD

I sometimes feel guilty for dreaming. *Is this selfish? Shouldn't we just focus completely on God and not get narcissistic, thinking there are special things we should all be doing? Just focus on God?*

Honestly, it is good to think about because we live in a time in church history when we have strategically justified obsessive amounts of self-focus. We have made life about our little stories rather than God's story. We have become a generation obsessed with understanding ourselves, as if that holds the answer for our restless, discontent souls.

We have come to treat God as if He exists for us, rather than us existing for Him. As if He is supposed to fit our plans, rather than our only plan being to know Him and to follow Him.

God is big, but He moves into the small. God cares about eternity, yet

He cares about every second of every human's life. That is who we serve. When God is *only* big and *only* about eternal heavenly things in our minds, we miss out. We stop dreaming before we even start because we fail to see how He could be interested. And we miss some key things.

We miss Jesus. When we believe God is only in the big, we miss that Jesus loved each individual deeply and met their unique needs. We miss how creatively He pursued each of us until we believed. We miss His vision for His church: one body, many unique parts coming together to make a difference with their small moments.

We miss His Spirit. Jesus sent a Helper to live in and through us, to pray for us, to equip us with unique gifts, to encourage us, and to remind us of our purpose here. And to remind us that we are headed to a home better than the one we will risk for Him now. We miss this beautiful, personal interaction with our living God if in our minds He stays only the distant Creator of planets.

We miss God's creativity. Just look around. Everything about you is different from every other human on earth. By design. God creates generations and billions of interesting humans, and then He takes time to write intimate and unique moments for each one of them.

Ignore this side of God, and you will miss the point: He ran after you. He wrote stories for you. He numbered your days. He knows your thoughts before you think them and your words before you speak them. Ignore that He adores you, and you might as well shrivel up and die and go to heaven to be with Him. He is big, and He moves into the small. It's God's dichotomy that makes Him so absolutely mind-blowing.

We miss the mystery of God. My favorite professor in seminary taught me the most painful and difficult truth about following God: *embrace the tension*.

I watch online as religious bloggers and theologians all fight for various values they hold dear. They are fighting on some deep level for what they believe is absolutely true of God. But they often pull so hard (God is this way and not that way) that they yank away the tension that maintains truth. Even humans can't be easily boxed in. And if we can't, God certainly can't be either.

Somehow, in His holy otherness, our God is . . .

- sovereign and has given us the freedom to make decisions;
- loving and just;
- the One who hates evil and yet has full authority over it and permits its existence;
- one God yet three all at once;
- and the One for whom time doesn't exist, yet He intentionally planned every moment of it for us.

And I could go on all day long.

We hate tension. We love to land somewhere, but this one little admonition—*embrace the tension*—keeps me humble, keeps God as God, and keeps me slightly capable of knowing a smidgen of Him. He is unknowable in so many ways, so mystery must be applied to our small understanding of Him and what He has revealed to us in Scripture. But we do know, through His Word and His Spirit, that He has given us enough. "His divine power has given us everything we need for a godly life" (2 Peter 1:3).

We often desperately chase knowledge of "God's will for me" at the sacrifice of God's will. We will not do that here. As we look into what our dreams might be, what our call might be, let's embrace the tension of seeking God's will for us, individually, within God's revealed will for this earth—for eternity and for His people. We won't ever stop searching for purpose until God's will becomes our passion.

RESPOND

So what were your dreams as a kid? What did you want to be? When did you stop dreaming?

Have you ever thought of God as a dreamer? What do you think His dreams are for us?

Did you ever have ridiculously big dreams for changing the world? Or highly "unrealistic" dreams that didn't occur to you as any kind of big deal? What were they?

In what ways are we "a generation obsessed with understanding ourselves"? How might understanding God be a better way for us to do that?

How does believing that God moves into the small help us understand

   a. what Jesus did?
   b. what the Spirit does?
   c. God's creativity?

READ & REFLECT

Read 2 Peter 1:3–11 as you think of embracing the tension involved in seeking God's will.

Why is it important to confirm our calling and understand it?

How could dreaming with a God who is both big and small keep you from becoming "nearsighted"?

After reading these passages, consider the answers to these two questions:

Who are You, Lord?

What do You want for me?

WHAT'S KEEPING US FROM DREAMING?

He chose us in him before the creation of the world
to be holy and blameless in his sight.

—EPHESIANS 1:4

What could cause us to miss God's plans? I think a lot of us are afraid. We've got hang-ups, and some of us have deep needs that we don't even have words for. Before we go any further, let's start thinking about what those might be.

To get our hearts primed and ready to begin dreaming, we need to till the soil a little. Loosen up the hard parts and make room for the seeds to grow. To do that, we'll confront our worries, fears, hang-ups, uncertainties, and misplaced motives, digging out the rocks and making a safe place for us to begin to dream again. There are so many things that keep us from dreaming, and we start to deal with them by opening up our mouths and letting the words out.

The Things That Stop Us

- "I honestly don't care about God."
- "I don't think God cares about me."

- "I'm afraid of what people will think."
- "I want a comfortable life."
- "My spouse won't be on board."
- "I think I'll fail."
- "I have nothing to give God."
- "I don't think my life even matters much."

I heard these words from women who had gathered with me at a church retreat in the Texas countryside. With raw honesty, they slowly let the words fall out. It was a safe place, and they were ready to deal with their hurt, sin, and anything stopping them from dreaming. Then, with all the mess of it pooling on the floor of our cabin, I looked around the room and saw a hint of something—a little sparkle, possible hope in their eyes.

As they spoke, the worries that had consumed each person moments before now looked miserably ridiculous staring back at them. The realization needed no words. We were faced with a simple, striking image: strong, resourced, rescued people who were full of God and going through life completely shut down by lies and fear.

Could there be more to life than this?

We were all certain that there was, and with all the chains on the floor, we could almost taste what we had been missing. We were about to remember what running with abandon felt like, what purpose felt like, what dreaming felt like, what freedom felt like.

Do you need to remember that there is more?

How to run freely?

What purpose feels like?

What freedom feels like?

Some of us have decorated our prison walls so beautifully that we have forgotten that we're sitting in a cell, wasting our lives. We don't know there are chains that, though they no longer bind us, still tangle us up. We sit and listen to talks or read books about God, and we wonder why nothing changes when we so desperately want it to. We forget that we have access to the exit door of that cell.

OUR TANGLED THREADS

You have threads of life blowing around, possibly even strangling you—threads meant to bind together and become your unique, God-given contribution to a world in great need. And not just for a world in need. Our souls were made to find their home in God with His purposes for our lives. But while your heart is aching for purpose, to know what those threads are, how to untangle them, and how they will weave together, I want to remind you: no unique purpose for your life will fill your soul. The only One who will fulfill and settle your soul is God Himself.

We tend to think that if we land on our perfect purpose, we will finally be satisfied. Hear me: we have complete access to joy and purpose right now. Even with no grand vision from God, we have access to our Creator, and He is not hiding happiness from us. He gave it to us in the form of Christ. Everything we are going to talk about is just a response to our God.

Our significance doesn't depend on a stellar performance. We matter because we are children of the living, breathing, reigning God of the universe. We matter because we were bought with the blood of the Son of our Father God. He "chose us in him before the creation of the world" (Eph. 1:4) and set us in our spots and in our time. He numbered our days and counts our hair. And we matter because He says we matter. This isn't a journey about you suddenly finding a secret way to matter; it's about realizing you *already* matter. You can deeply desire to make your few days here count in light of all that is ahead for us as children of such a God. That realization—that's the open door to the cell we've built. That's what makes us confront what's been consuming us.

SET FREE

I've wasted a lot of my life. I grew up in a sickening chase to win people's approval—approval that I could never catch. And so I gave most of my life to the cause of being liked. God was never enough for me.

It's not a noble cause. It's embarrassing, I know. But chances are that you aren't noble either, and you've likely wasted your life on . . . something.

But what if we just stop? What if we wake up? We are building mansions on sand when an enormous, steadfast, unmovable rock sits right beside us. For years I ran after uncatchable wind and built homes on sand until I finally noticed that wind never stops escaping us and sand never stops shifting.

I was consumed with pride and self. I saw my sin, and God saved my soul. He set me free. And now all of us who love God are in it together, fighting to stay free and to free people around us because there is a God who never escapes us and never shifts. Everywhere I go, people's eyes contain hurt similar to what mine did.

Is God real?
Do I matter?
Is there more than this?
Is this all worth it?

Yes. I swear it.

RESPOND

If you were to get brutally honest about the hurts stopping you from dreaming, what words would fall out?

How might sharing those words help you see them differently?

In what ways can listening and learning about God while holding on to these worries be like "decorating your cell"?

How is it freeing to believe "this isn't a journey about you suddenly finding a secret way to matter; it's about realizing you already matter"?

What does our significance depend on? What does it not depend on?

READ & REFLECT

Read Ephesians 1:3–14 as you think about your responses to today's questions.

In light of these verses, why do we matter?

How are we set free?

What is the purpose of knowing God's will?

After reading these passages, consider the answers to these two questions:

Who are You, Lord?

What do You want for me?

DAY 9

SURRENDER IS SCARY

I say to you, unless a grain of wheat falls into the earth and dies, it remains alone; but if it dies, it bears much fruit. Whoever loves his life loses it, and whoever hates his life in this world will keep it for eternal life.

—JOHN 12:24–25 ESV

A seed comes from the living flesh of a fruit. But it will never be more than a hard nuisance that gets stuck in our teeth unless it is buried in the ground. And even then, in the dark, it is encased in a thick shell—dead and hard. But under the dirt, flesh is birthed out of something lifeless. It breaks through and pushes to the surface; it moves and grows, running up and out of something that was dead. Now it's alive—now it brings life.

See, the life I want so badly lies on the other side of death.

The life you want lies on the other side of death.

That death is also called *surrender.*

Still, we think, *I can't let go of control of my normal because it requires a little death. I know that tightening my grip will strangle what I'm holding, but I'm afraid of the sting that little death will produce.* We're afraid to let go, but we'll start seeing the hope in it all once our hearts are set on God's dreams.

We are going to dream God's dreams here. Maybe you started this journey with some idea of what you hope to dream about—a small business or a noble cause to save the world—and we will get there. But as Bill Bright, the founder of Campus Crusade for Christ, used to teach, until there is surrender, there is no vision.[1] And Proverbs says, "Where there is no vision, the people perish" (29:18 KJV).

We've talked about how scary it is to pray *anything*, handing over every dream for our lives—every hope, every remnant of control we think we have—to God, and we say, "You have all of it. You have me. I am Yours. Anything You want to do with me. Anything. I am in."

I'm serious. It is terrifying. But it's essential to go back there again before we begin. We were bought with an enormous price, and it is no longer we who live, but Christ who lives in us (1 Cor. 6:20; Gal. 2:20). So if we don't begin with surrender, we inevitably dream with vanity, with ego, with control.

The scariest and safest thing I have ever done is pray this *anything* prayer—to hand complete control of my life and my dreams over to my God. We all have hopes of how our lives will turn out, and we all fear that if God actually has His way with us, He may slingshot us to the other side of the world or, worse, ask us to share Christ with the person in the house or cubicle next to ours. We are scared that God's dreams for us may not be as cool as the ones we create.

We who are saved have been set apart for a great purpose—and that great purpose is actually not a secret: we are to know God and make Him known. So we do not dream independently, and God does not sign off on our dreams. He is the builder of our dreams. We bring Him our blank canvases, hand them over, and say, "Whatever You must create to display Your glory, do it."

BETTER DREAMS

I do not lightly ask you to pray for surrender. We begin this process as every creator begins: with a blank canvas, hoping that something beautiful is about to come into being. But I have to tell you, there have been days when I have seen God painting pictures through our lives that I would give anything to paint over with my own brushstrokes. But we can't know what the picture will turn out to be. Like any great artist, we have to be open to the mystery of inspiration: God creating something through us.

One of the most basic human questions is: "What is God's will for my life?" We are going to have so much fun answering this question. *But* until you are all in, you'll be capable of dreaming only your own inadequate and small dreams. Because we are never free until we let go.

THE BEAUTIFUL EXCHANGE

If you feel too weary to dream—if you feel too empty to give—you are in good company. But with the ache for "easy" comes a whisper of bigger things. Know this: whatever God does with our lives, He is good and is fighting for us in the most noble ways; He gave His Son's life to win us back. So might He pour our lives out in difficult ways? Yes. But He is the God of planets and my soul. He gave everything for us. So I will entrust my entire life to no one else. We surrender to a God who surrendered everything for us.

I trust Him. He came down from heaven to get to us. He is worthy of our surrender. How ridiculous for me to want to paint my own story.

Great people do not do great things; God does great things through surrendered people. If I breathe on this earth for a few more decades, I would rather lose everything temporary for anything that is permanent.

We make a beautiful exchange:

- Our short lives for forever.
- Our moving sand for the rock of a God who adores us.

- Our chains for running wild and free.
- Our chasing after the wind for a purpose that will never fade.

We get to dream. We get to live our lives worthy of the most amazing calling. As much as I want an umbrella drink by an ocean somewhere, I just as much want to never waste a minute of life.

Can you pray, "God, anything. You have me"? If so, this is about to get fun.

RESPOND

Respond to the idea that "we do not dream independently, and God does not sign off on our dreams. He is the builder of our dreams." How is that freeing? How is that scary?

Why can we trust God enough to surrender to Him?

What holds us back from trusting Him in this way?

From your life or from the Bible, how have you witnessed that "great people do not do great things; God does great things through surrendered people"?

Have you ever felt too weary to dream? How can giving up control give us hope?

READ & REFLECT

Read John 12:20–28 as you think about your responses to today's questions.

In what context did Jesus say these words about seeds and dying? What was He predicting?

According to verse 25, what do we gain and how?

In verses 27–28, how did Jesus feel about becoming this seed, and what did He do about it?

After reading these passages, consider the answers to these two questions:

Who are You, Lord?

What do You want for me?

WHY ARE WE AFRAID OF OURSELVES?

*Whoever believes in me will also do the works that I
do; and greater works than these will he do.*

—JOHN 14:12 ESV

Recently, I asked a string of questions on Facebook: "How do your motives hold you back from running headfirst into God's purposes for you? Should they hold us back? Or are we paralyzed by fear of ourselves?"

The conversation that exploded in the comment section of this post exposed that I wasn't the only one who was terrified of myself.

We are afraid of big dreams because we are afraid of ourselves.

We are afraid of greatness because we are afraid of our arrogance.

And yet Jesus said of us, "Whoever believes in me . . . they will do even greater things than these" (John 14:12). It almost sounds blasphemous to do even greater things. We rarely say it, but when we start to have hints of great thoughts or visions, we often quickly dismiss them, afraid that we may be vain. Arrogant. Prideful. Or worse, simply that we would *appear* prideful.

Ambition is complicated. *Bigger. More.* When related to material things it sounds like greed, so we often take the idea of "bigger and more" in our lives and boil it all down to sin. We sit in the back like my friend Jamie, who aches to dream but says, "It always seems easier to sit on the back row and kill my dreams than to fight the sin that may be attached to those dreams."

I fight these wars in my soul nearly every day. For so long I just sat in the back, my dreams spilling out on the floor. But then I found myself in a room with a woman who did not seem to know how to dream small. She is a giant in the world of ministry, and we had the afternoon to ask any questions of her that we wanted. With a big vision growing in my heart, I knew exactly what I wanted to ask: "How do you know if a vision is from God?"

She looked down and then directly and simply said, "At some point you look at the motives of your heart, and if they are for God, then just do it."

It was simple and difficult all at the same time because a convoluted mixture of motives undergirds every pursuit in life.

AFRAID OF ARROGANCE

As Zac and I prayed, "God, we will do anything," I knew the reason I had not been using my gifts in any great capacity was because I was afraid of appearing arrogant. When I was an eighteen-year-old, I knew I had the gift of teaching and I knew how to lead. For years I taught younger women in my living room. I looked around our community and saw so many women who needed more of God. Though I had great ideas of how to give Him to them, I was paralyzed with this fear. Beginning a small Bible study in our church seems like no big deal now, but it was a painfully scary thought then.

I remember telling myself things like, *I will humbly sit in the back and give other people the chance to lead*. It sounds good. But I was completely disobeying God, and I wasn't playing the part in the body of Christ that

God had designed me to play. Because by using my gifts, others would be released to use their gifts, and so on.

We need to quit apologizing for using our gifts and start apologizing for *not* using them. I would say to myself, *I am ministering to younger girls in my living room. That is enough. Greatness isn't in size.*

Of course it would have been enough, if God wasn't calling me to something more. Some people charge mountains with no fear of themselves, and they need to check their motives. Some never take a mountain because of too much fear of themselves, and checking those motives is just as important.

God exposed my false humility. Nervously, with the support of our church leaders, I offered my first public study, *Stuck*, to our small church plant. Somehow 150 women found their way to a little cafeteria, and I taught them how God designed the spaces within us to be full of only Him. Christians' lives were turning upside down; some even wondered if they had ever truly been saved. Unbelievers found safety, and a dozen people received Christ in the months that followed. God had been wanting to move through me, and I had never let Him because I was worried I would appear arrogant.

AFRAID OF CRITICISM

Near the end of that study, after watching God work in the most unbelievable ways, two people in the study voiced criticism about the very fears that had paralyzed me before: my motives. As I processed their criticism, I began to spin. Yes, the thing I most feared was happening. I had stepped out and led in our community, and I was potentially coming off as arrogant to people I cared about. I craved a return to the safety of the back row and the anonymity it once had given me.

As I shared the hurt from this with my friend Karen, rather than comfort me with all the good things that God had done, she simply asked me, "Is God pleased with you in this?"

Everything in me quit spinning, and with 100 percent certainty I answered, "Yes, He is."

I knew how difficult the last few months had been. In faith I had acted in obedience, pushing through my fears of approval to lead for His name's sake and for people's healing and freedom. I knew that God was pleased. I could not say that my motives were in the right place at other times in my life, but this time I had complete peace.

Then Karen said, "Then what else is there?"

At the core of our souls lie our volitions, our wills, our deepest desires. Karen asked me a question she could not know the answer to. She asked me to reveal something that mere results, criticism, visible greatness, or failure cannot reveal. She asked me if my motives were pure. She asked me if my heart was right before my God.

Every one of us was made to do great things, which is why something in us feels restless and discontent. Deep down we know we were created for some great purpose. And these great things we were built to do are for God, through God, and in God.

I know sometimes it feels impossible to sort out the heart. Let's decide together that we can and will push through the fears that keep us from moving into all that God has planned for us.

RESPOND

Have you ever stopped yourself from something because you were afraid to *appear* prideful?

When it comes to criticism, are you able to tell the difference between what people think and what God thinks?

How do you know if God is pleased with you?

Have you ever apologized for using your gifts or for stepping out into a dream?

In what area have you shrunk back when you think perhaps God was wanting to move through you?

READ & REFLECT

Read John 14:11–21, keeping in mind your responses to today's questions.

Right after Jesus said we would do greater works, who did He promise to send to us? Why?

In verse 11, who do the works point to? How could adopting this attitude keep us from shrinking back and killing our dreams?

After reading these passages, consider the answers to these two questions:

Who are You, Lord?
What do You want for me?

PURELY DEVOTED

If I were still trying to please people, I would not be a servant of Christ.

—GALATIANS 1:10

The truth is, the fear of greatness originates in the right place, since we usually do struggle to have the right motives. Most of us would love to make a name for ourselves, and we spend a lot of our energy trying, but at the same time trying not to look like we are trying.

We were built for the greatness of God. But left to ourselves, we love being great more than we love making God great. So whether you are building up your own name, or you are just too scared to build anything because you don't want to look egotistical, both mind-sets are wrong.

I have talked to enough of you to know that many of you are sitting on your gifts too. The Enemy is subtle and warps truths into lies for us. He tells us we are being humble, responsible, and selfless, while we are killing the things God put us on the planet to do, the things that would build His kingdom.

We live in a world in love with fame. Almost anyone who works hard enough can find a way to get noticed and to make money doing so. Unfortunately, this is true as much in Christendom as it is anywhere. And while it is not our responsibility to judge anyone else's motives, it is very much our responsibility to scrutinize our own. And it's a good idea to do so daily. While most days I drag my heels in following more public callings, when others start applauding me, all of a sudden I start waving and loving it. We all fight our divided motives every day. The key is to *fight*.

So how do we fight? Whether you are building a name for yourself or sitting on the back row hiding so people won't judge you, the answer is the same: *we get over ourselves*.

FLOURISH

Soon no name on this earth will matter but one. Not yours, not mine. That one name has asked you to build with Him. And who wouldn't trade building sand castles to get to build something that lasts forever?

Paul wrote, "If I were still trying to please people, I would not be a servant of Christ" (Gal. 1:10). Western mentality has shaped our views of work and success and calling so deeply that it is difficult to shake the idea of pleasing and impressing other people. God is asking us to get over it. And shift our thinking.

We see big and small. We see secular and Christian. We see size and numbers. We decide what constitutes "important work." It feels impossible to sort out motives; it takes so much energy to go around with yardsticks, measuring and comparing and weighing everything.

Tim Keller defines meaningful work as taking the raw materials we are given and assembling them in a way that causes other people to flourish.[1] For instance, a gifted composer takes individual notes that alone just sound like noise, until she assembles them into something beautiful that causes others to flourish. Authors and artists do the same with words, paint, or clay.

Now what about less creative, seemingly more mundane work? A housekeeper takes chaos and assembles order so that others will flourish in that environment. An accountant takes numbers and assembles them so that others can pay their taxes and flourish by avoiding prison. Mothers take the raw materials of their children and shape them into people who will one day help others flourish.

Good work. Hard work. Helping others. Those things have always been noble. Those things have always been respected.

But the game has changed for us. Somehow we have assembled different scales that weigh titles and incomes and even the amount of sacrifice a particular action requires. Some college students told me that their friends all compete to do the most sacrificial things with their summers. Apparently it's as if you are sinful if you aren't going to a third-world country. We have hijacked the game, measuring worth with a scale that God did not create. Doing things for the applause of others, we muddy our purposes.

Personal fulfillment is fullest when we are involved in something bigger than ourselves, something for the good of others. We can either be looking for our own glory or involved in the master plan. Competing for praise or settled on the good of others.

What if we took the pieces of our lives (no matter what the world says they are worth) and began to use them to help others flourish for the sake of Christ? All of a sudden our motives would narrow to contain more of God and others, and less of us.

Is it so wrong to want to make a big impact with your days here, for God?

EMBRACING THORNS

That gut-check in our motives can be used for good instead of stopping us in our tracks.

I used to watch people in the limelight of ministry with a bit of jealousy. They seemed to be magically using their gifts and seemed so fulfilled—so happy. They appeared to be honoring God, and then as an added bonus, to possess all of our respect and admiration. *How rewarding*, I thought. Until . . . that light shined on me just a little.

In our ministry, scrutiny and opinions have found us. Battling Satan . . . not really a highlight. And juggling the weight of leading people to God—while trying to pull off godly mom and wife and friend and car-pool driver . . . heavy balls to toss around.

See, God has a means of shaping our motives. He wants our hearts to be pure. He is changing us, humbling us, making our hearts beat for Him.

Paul told us about a thorn in his flesh (2 Cor. 12:7–9). Thorns push us to need God, and as I make my way through my thorns, my motives, I remember my humanity, my insecurity, my fear, my sin. But I know if it were easier, I'd go looking for the limelight instead of for God.

What if we just ran despite our thorns and our sin and let God straighten us out as we go? We can't wait until our sin is gone before we run, or we never will. We have to fight it *as* we run. I think in twenty years we will regret more of the things we didn't do than the things we did imperfectly.

RESPOND

Have you ever stepped out and done something imperfectly and been really glad you did? What was it like?

Can you think of any scales you use to measure worth in this world—scales that God did not create?

Have you ever weighed a dream on that scale and found it wanting?

What do you do right now that helps others flourish?

Why do we sit on our gifts? How might embracing our thorns help us get up off them?

READ & REFLECT

Read Galatians 1:6–24, keeping in mind your answers to today's questions.

How is the Western mentality of work and success (or the American dream) like a "different gospel"?

In the story Paul told of his origins in verses 11–24, how was God glorified through a messy, imperfect story?

After reading these passages, consider the answers to these two questions:

Who are You, Lord?
What do You want for me?

EMBRACING UNCERTAINTIES

*No eye has seen, no ear has heard, and no mind has imagined
what God has prepared for those who love him.*

—1 CORINTHIANS 2:9 NLT

We face so many uncertainties in life. Especially when deciding whether to step out into a dream—or even dream in the first place. Not knowing if we're on the right track can stop us before we start. But don't be afraid to ask the big questions. Whatever the answer is, we can trust that God has prepared something good for us. You may be asking:

STAY OR GO?

I used to think missionaries were the only fully surrendered superheroes of the faith. The truly godly sold all they owned and lived in huts somewhere. The next-highest level of superheroes committed to vocational ministry in the United States. This thought now makes me sick to write because the most surrendered people I know are living normal lives, helping the people who come into their paths in profound ways. Physicians. Waiters.

Entrepreneurs. Stay-at-home moms. Builders. Landscapers. They're doing the things that God put them on earth to do. If they asked the question "Is this about us or about God?" they'd know without a doubt their answer: God.

However, some have prayed and given their lives, and they *were* called to go:

- Our good friends Gloria and Dave Furman began the first evangelical, English-speaking Christian church in downtown Dubai. They obeyed and left every comfort of a familiar culture, and God is using them to impact one of the most influential parts of the world.
- Our friends Bill and Lisa Miller knew they could take their love for God into Prague but not as vocational ministers, so he is a professor at a local college. With his gifts and training, they have seen many people come to Christ.

So do you stay or do you go? I do not know. I am not telling you to move. And I am not telling you to stay. Just to say, "God, have Your way."

SMALL OR BIG?

I can't tell the difference between what the world thinks is big or small and what God thinks is big or small because it is the wrong question, and I rarely ask it anymore.

The only question to ask here is "What am I supposed to do, God?" And then do it. Don't analyze it; just do it.

In the coming days you'll find out more about how Joseph knew God deeply and trusted Him. So much of his life was seemingly inconsequential, like scrubbing floors in Potiphar's house. But to him, scrubbing a floor with excellence mattered to God. Staring at a prison wall for years mattered because it was building the character of a man who would forgive the evil of his brothers, and who ultimately—and most importantly—would lead a country out of ruin.

In our culture we judge with backward values and twisted motives. We love to make stars out of people and then watch them fall. We do this for sport. And then we crave that stardom that is so obviously not fulfilling. An old saying goes, "Do what you love and the money will follow." I don't know if you will love what God calls you to do (you might), and I certainly can't promise that money will follow (it may). But I can tell you that at the end of our lives, when we stand before God, these are the only things that will matter:

- Did I do what God wanted me to be doing while I was here?
- Did I complete the works He had for me?
- Did I fulfill my purposes in my generation?

So instead of waiting until we're standing in God's throne room, let's work backward and ask those questions now. Let's live them today. Not for salvation that can't be earned but in response to God, who built and rescued us as part of His great purpose. If you are willing, He will lead you.

Small or big? It's so relative. If we compare ourselves to others, what they are doing can shrink our important roles till they seem insignificant. Comparison robs us of the joy of obedience.

When you're feeling small, know that the most inconspicuous tasks are usually building big things we can't see yet.

VOCATION OR CALLING?

Are we talking about our jobs or our callings here? In many ways, this is a similar question to the small or big question. And it has a similar answer.

For some of us, our careers are our callings, and we live out our callings while doing a job. It is a rare gift to pay your bills as you fill up your soul. For most of the world and most every generation, work is about provision, not personal fulfillment. There is enough personal satisfaction in being able to feed your family.

Within the Western world we have the luxury of millions of jobs in almost as many fields—even in times of economic crisis—and yet sometimes people complain about their unsatisfying jobs for years. Personally, I want to shake them and say, "We live in a world where you can change your job. Change it, for crying out loud!"

But sometimes we are called to stay in our places, even if it is the most mind-numbing, miserable thing in the world. This is about something deeper than a job (and we'll talk more about it later), yet we can't ignore our jobs. This is about how we spend our minutes and our days. Because eventually our minutes and days equal our lives.

God calls people to all types of vocations. For example, David was a warrior and then a king. Nehemiah was a cupbearer and then a wall-builder. Daniel and Joseph were counselors to national leaders, Jesus was a carpenter before His life in ministry, and Paul was a tentmaker. There are no such things as spiritual and secular jobs—we made that up. God calls people to Himself, and then calls us to display Him in every way, wherever we are. So are you called to teach or write or mother or build homes or fly planes? Beautiful. Do it as unto the Lord.

God works—He builds and creates. He sees chaos and brings order, and His work is characterized by joy and service to us. You were made to create and build and reflect His image.

Work was given as a gift before the fall; we weren't made to sit around and do nothing. We were made to work in the mundane, but we aren't defined by the mundane. Because Jesus set us apart with a deep purpose to live out as we teach or write or mother or build homes or fly planes, there is no difference between a vocation and a calling. If you're showing God to the world in whatever job you're doing, you're on the right track.

RESPOND

Has uncertainty ever stopped you from embracing a dream? How/when?

How have small callings or tasks led to bigger things in your life?

When it comes to callings and dreams, are big and small ultimately any different? How or how not?

Reflect on the idea that "the most inconspicuous tasks are usually building big things we can't see yet." What inconspicuous tasks are you engaged in?

Has work ever felt mundane for you? What does it mean to you that "we were made to work in the mundane, but we aren't defined by the mundane"?

READ & REFLECT

Read 1 Corinthians 2:6–16 as you think about your answers to today's questions.

How could some of the small callings or mundane things of life be considered like the "foolishness" the world sees in verse 14?

How does the person with the Spirit judge such things?

How does verse 7 describe God's wisdom? How can that help in our uncertainties?

After reading these passages, consider the answers to these two questions:

Who are You, Lord?

What do You want for me?

WHAT WE CAN KNOW
AND WHAT WE CAN'T

Do not neglect the gift you have.

—1 TIMOTHY 4:14 ESV

I read a book recently that I really appreciate; its message was to quit analyzing everything and just *do* something.[1] I couldn't agree more. As a
culture we are obsessed with analyzing ourselves and talking about ourselves, when at the end of the day, people are sick and dying. People don't
know God. People are enslaved. We are going though divorces and depression and burying children while we are figuring ourselves out!

I do believe, however, that for a short—and I mean a *short*—season we
can pull back and consider specifically what God may want from us here.
As Zac and I were fumbling our way through seminary, we honestly did
not know exactly why we were there. So we began the process of uncover-
ing our unique place in God's plans. It felt like navel-gazing. I was nervous
it was selfish, and I even resisted at first. As I was asking God for peace
about this season of self-discovery, I remembered a professor teaching us
that you truly can't help anyone else until you understand yourself better.

This will not be self-analysis for the sake of inner fulfillment, though

I believe deeper joy is a by-product. This is about understanding the story of God and how to play our parts in it, to serve Him and His people while we are here. We are going to be learning new things, but know that God is already at work. We can't wait until we've got it all figured out. Continue to respond to things where you are. Because it's often as you go, as you trust God, that direction is confirmed.

When John Piper was asked how we find the will of God for our lives, he replied to know Scripture, know yourself, and know the need around you.[2] It is all right to know yourself, especially for the sake of God and others. Scripture supports this again and again:

> God has placed the parts in the body, every one of them, just as he wanted them to be. If they were all one part, where would the body be? As it is, there are many parts, but one body. (1 Cor. 12:18–20)

> Do not neglect the gift you have. (1 Tim. 4:14 ESV)

> To each is given the manifestation of the spirit for the common good. (1 Cor. 12:7 ESV)

There is a time and a place to search for our unique parts in God's story, *but* . . . here is my challenge to you:

Respond to the need you see. *Right now.*

"Give to everyone who asks you" (Luke 6:30). We are called to care for the things we see right in front of us, and anything else we can touch, regardless of our wiring and stories. As we live out our callings, we respond to need no matter what. So don't bother waiting around for a unique voice to come out of the sky. We move, respond, love, and obey. And as we go, God leads humble souls who are willing to be led.

WHAT GOD HAS PREPARED

My middle sister, Brooke, and her husband, Tony, run a guest ranch in Colorado called Lost Valley Ranch. They lead dozens of young staff, who beautifully host dozens of guests every week. On one of my visits to the ranch, the head chef, Matt, walked out of the kitchen to find me. We had never met, but I knew exactly who he was. He was coming to thank me. One insignificant and unknowing moment of my life had changed his, and he wanted to shake my hand.

Three years earlier, I sat in my car outside of Bible study with a young girl named Anne. She was twenty-two and finished with college, and as she watched her friends accepting jobs and making wedding plans, she felt lost. She wondered aloud what direction her life should take; the railroad tracks of the last twenty-two years had ended, and now she was forced to build her own track.

She was restless and uncertain, but she sat in my car holding on to a few things that only equaled confusion in her mind.

She loved to cook, and she was good at it.

She had clear gifts of hospitality and leadership.

She wanted to use these things to minister.

As she talked, I wrote the name of the ranch and my sister's name and phone number on a scrap of paper. Anne hopped out of the car, and the next thing I knew, my sister and her husband had hired her for the summer. The summer turned into three years, and waitressing turned into running the kitchen, and a cute chef turned into a fiancé named Matt.

The day I met Matt, we sat talking about God's brilliant planning. That night in my car, Anne didn't have even a hint of her future. But God had already written the story, and He placed that restless feeling in her that made her ask for a moment of my time. He gave her enough knowledge of herself to lead her to a unique place, hundreds of miles from home, where He was writing another story that would eventually intersect with hers.

> "No eye has seen, no ear has heard,
>   and no mind has imagined
> what God has prepared
>   for those who love him." (1 Cor. 2:9 NLT)

God is accomplishing a thousand tiny purposes at any given moment around us. There is only so much we can know, but we can leave the stuff we can't know to God and believe He has it all worked out. It may feel quiet, and we possibly even feel forgotten, but God is moving to work out His plans all around us.

What is our part?

Trust.

RESPOND

What's the value of analyzing ourselves?

What are the pitfalls of overanalyzing ourselves?

What makes understanding our part in God's story different from navel-gazing?

How does responding to need keep us from overanalyzing?

Looking back, can you pinpoint a situation when you wish you had asked, "Is this about me or about God"? What situation are you in right now that could be helped by this question?

READ & REFLECT

Read 1 Timothy 4:14–16, keeping in mind your answers to today's questions, Why should we watch our life and doctrine (i.e., analyze ourselves)?

What's the value of being "diligent in these matters"? Who witnesses the process?

After reading these passages, consider the answers to these two questions:

Who are You, Lord?
What do You want for me?

FOUR STARTING PLACES

There is a time for everything, and a season
for every activity under the heavens.

—ECCLESIASTES 3:1

We all come into this search for greater purpose from different places, and all of us will need different things through this process. This road will be unique to every person who goes through this experience. Can you see yourself in any of the following types of people?

COMFORTABLE

You don't know if you are living on purpose or not. You are busy and surviving and somewhat content. Maybe sometimes you are bored, but, in general, your life is full and you aren't one to overanalyze. Maybe you are beginning to wake up and hurt for more, but even that sentence just made you nervous.

Questions You May Be Asking

- Shouldn't I just feel thankful for what I have instead of wanting more?

- What is wrong with being comfortable and happy?
- Isn't it enough just to be faithful where I am?

To you, I would say this: "There is a time for everything. . . . A time to search and a time to give up . . . a time to tear and a time to mend, a time to be silent and a time to speak," and on and on (Eccl. 3:1, 6–7).

CARRIE'S STORY

Carrie wrote in to tell me that she'd started this journey from a place of comfort and contentment but discovered something she didn't expect:

> When I picked up *Restless*, I was not restless. In fact, I was fairly sure that I was doing what God had for me at that moment in life. I was fulfilled in my day-to-day responsibilities and overall felt contented. Going through the exercises laid out in *Restless* was not only an encouragement, but even more a confirmation of paths that I had chosen to pursue.
>
> So after doing the study, when I was asked what had stolen my joy in recent months, I was completely confused. I had felt so confirmed in what I was pursuing that I had not noticed the discontent that had crept in. I had no answer. And that sent me to my knees. What the Lord showed me were deep-seated idols that I had long ago hidden from myself. Without the intentionality of the *Restless* study, I would have second-guessed the paths I was pursuing instead of digging deeper to the heart issues affecting life and joy in Christ.

Comfortable can become uncomfortable in the best way. This may be your time to tear up and your time to search and speak and consider. For a short season I want you to consider that there may be more. Because I would rather you be unsettled for a minute, and sure that you are in the will of God, than content in the wrong place.

THIRSTY

You hurt. Inside you are longing for more. You are begging for a clearer purpose than you currently feel. But you don't know if your restless heart is the Enemy making you unsettled, or your friend pushing you toward greater things. You are not satisfied, but you don't know what to do about it. You are asking yourself, "Is there more? And if there is, how do I find it?"

Questions You May Be Asking

- Is it wrong to want more?
- Does God have some secret purpose that I am missing?
- What if there is no clear direction?

The apostle Paul wrote from prison, "I urge you to live a life worthy of the calling you have received" (Eph. 4:1). There remained a restlessness in Paul throughout his life. He urgently went about the work of God and asked us to do the same. I don't know if your restless heart is sinful or from God. But I do know that God often awakens and moves me toward more with a deep discontentment and an unsettling feeling of dissatisfaction. Many times when I longed for more, sure enough, He had more for me. We will deal with all of these questions, so don't preach away that restlessness yet.

RUNNING FREE

Some of you are living it. You feel purpose. You are running hard after God and are being obedient, and you have watched God move around you. You know what you are made to do, and perhaps you are already doing it. You have already moved through a season of feeling numb or satisfied, and you've become restless and found more. Life is full and hard, but rich and fulfilling too.

Questions You May Be Asking

- Do I even need this?
- I already know the answers to a lot of these questions, so why should I keep reading?

Let us throw off everything that hinders and the sin that so easily entangles. And let us run with perseverance the race marked out for us, fixing our eyes on Jesus, the pioneer and perfecter of faith . . . so that you will not grow weary and lose heart. (Heb. 12:1–3)

Some of my friends who are running the hardest have said they need this journey more than anyone else because we all forget. I have been in all three places over and over again, and you will too. We start running the race we were meant to run, and then we realize after mile five that we have accidentally signed up for a marathon. And before we know it, we are bored or restless all over again. I pray these words would hand you water on your run. Let them fill you with new strength and focus. Let them remind you afresh of your calling so you will keep running and not grow weary. We are not home yet, and I pray that this journey will help you persevere in your race.

AT THE STARTING LINE

Or maybe you've realized that you don't really know God, that you don't actually have a personal relationship with Him, where you talk every day and you look to Him and live for Him. If that's the case, before you go any further, read the "How to Find God" page in the back of this book. It'll be the best, most important thing you'll ever do.

———

We are about to begin the process of identifying the unique threads God has given you, but before we begin it is important you reflect on where you start this process.

RESPOND

Take a minute alone and pray before you move ahead. Then take a few minutes before God and write out your answers to the questions below.

Which of these stages do you most relate to right now? Why?

    a. Numb
    b. Thirsty
    c. Running Free
    d. At the Starting Line

Does anything about wanting "more" make you nervous? Why or why not?

What stops you from running full steam ahead? From dreaming? From obeying? Respond to these questions in relation to each category below:

- Physical (examples: time, energy, finances, responsibilities, health)

- Emotional (examples: depression, fear, insecurity)

- Relational (examples: tension, hurt from childhood, discouragement)

- Spiritual (examples: belief, motives, strongholds, sin, shame)

READ & REFLECT

Read Ecclesiastes 3:1–14, keeping in mind your answers to today's questions.

Looking at the list of "a time to" in verses 2–8, do you currently identify with any of these actions in your journey toward discovering your purpose in God?

What is our relationship with eternity? How can that help us run our race from where we are?

What do we gain from our toil? Why is it a "gift from God"?

After reading these passages, consider the answers to these two questions:

Who are You, Lord?
What do You want for me?

PART 3

THE THREADS

THE PROCESS

Here is a boy with five small barley loaves and two small fish, but how far will they go among so many?

—JOHN 6:9

A rarely discussed secret is that almost all of us flail through our twenties. And one big reason is that we don't know ourselves yet. We are just barely learning . . .

- what we are good at,
- what we are terrible at,
- how our stories could ever be helpful to others,
- how to follow the Holy Spirit,
- how to not be a selfish brat,
- how to really love, and
- what our passions are.

But to be perfectly fair, I meet people all the time who are fifty-plus and still trying to figure it out.

Before we go any further, we have to understand what raw materials we have been given. These materials—what I've referred to before as threads—are given to us by God and for God. And we were built to run wild with them, so it is a valuable process to uncover and untangle them.

This idea can also be put into a simple equation:

God's Story + my threads + the need +
the Holy Spirit = my purpose.

Or to take it further:

The story of God through Scripture + an understanding of myself and my resources + taking inventory of the need around me + the mystery of following the Holy Spirit's leading = obediently living on purpose.

WHAT DO YOU HOLD?

I hope you will build a working understanding of the ways you have been created, the stories you have been given, the passions in your soul, the people in your path, the places you are to be, and the purposes the Holy Spirit is calling you toward.

When Jesus was about to do one of the most notable and beautiful miracles of His life here, He looked around and saw that thousands of people were hungry. Then, rather than create something out of nothing (which He was obviously capable of), He essentially said to His disciples, "Does anyone have any food?"[1]

One of the disciples found a little boy with a few fish and loaves of bread, and Jesus fed thousands with the few materials. That little boy had something of value in his hands: it was a starting place. It was the something that great things could be birthed from.

We hold things. We don't think much about it, but there are hungry people all around us, and God is looking to take the seemingly insignificant little pieces tucked away in our lives to multiply them and feed His people.

This journey is a chance to lay out what you have and what you know, and hand it up to God. I should mention: we have no idea what He will say to do, but we begin by laying it out and handing it over.

WHY DOES IT MATTER?

We want to live our lives intentionally. Without some effort, we will waste our minutes, our days . . . our lives. So putting thought into intentionally spending our time and resources for the glory of God may be the most important thing we will do with our lives.

As we understand ourselves in light of God's purposes, we are . . .

- moved to action,
- able to filter opportunities as they present themselves,
- equipped with a compass pointing toward God's purposes for our lives,
- and convicted that we are a part of a bigger story.

WHAT DO YOU NEED?

Prayer. Ask God to lead this process for you, to bring to mind memories, and to give supernatural insight and discernment as you process these important subjects.

People Who Know You. Gather together a few friends or family members who know you. Family can help you process and remember events from your past, and they can remind you of what you were great at as a kid. You also need friends who can speak truth into this process and hold you accountable as you move in faith. Gather everyone and ask them if you can do this together.

Reflection. As I said earlier, you are about to interact. So if you are reading this on your phone, get a journal and a pen. Even if you are reading a physical book, you will likely need more space to process than we could provide. You should not read this without responding in written form somewhere.

All these things will help you get moving and support you as you deal with the fear that inevitably comes from stepping out like this. Remember, "Twenty years from now you will be more disappointed by the things that you didn't do than by the ones you did do . . . Sail away from the safe harbor. Catch the trade winds in your sails. Explore. Dream. Discover."[2]

No greater question sits deep in our souls as humans than *"Why am I here?"*

But most of us can't answer it with any conviction for ourselves, even those of us who know God. Perhaps we could take a stab at why humans are here—but *why did God take the time to craft my days and life?* That one gets tricky. We hope we aren't accidents, and we try to believe that God has brilliantly diverse and specific purposes for our short lives here. But we don't know what they are, and deep down I think most of us doubt.

Let's tackle that weighty question. But before we do, take some time and process where you find yourself today in this journey.

RESPOND

What's the first thing that comes to mind when you think about the idea that you are holding something for other people?

Do you believe Jesus could do something with what little you have?

Which of your friends, family, and/or church family will you choose to help you in this process? Write their names here, and commit to asking them for help.

Collect your supplies and turn to the first page of your journal. Write a sentence or two about your motivation for going through this process, or write down your biggest questions. You could start by reflecting on "Why am I here?" "Why did God make me?" or "Why do I want to find out?"

How might a little bit of effort in this change your life at this stage?

READ & REFLECT

Read John 6:1–14, keeping in mind your answers to today's questions.

How did what the boy held glorify God?

What was the disciples' initial reaction to what he held?

How did the boy's story fit the "God's Story + my threads + the need + the Holy Spirit = my purpose" formula?

After reading these passages, consider the answers to these two questions:

Who are You, Lord?

What do You want for me?

THE PROJECT

Joseph had a dream.

—GENESIS 37:5

The story of our lives is adding up. What story will we tell? Of course, pictures and tweets could never tell the real story. The most sacred moments of our lives are bottled inside us—the moments that flash in our minds when our souls have never been so satisfied or the moments we wish we could forget because we have never felt so much pain. *These* are the actual stories of our lives. That sounded a little like the opening to *Days of Our Lives*—but you get it. Most of these moments go unreported and unanalyzed.

TANGLED UP

From an early age, Joseph had dreams and revelations from God. He specifically dreamed that his brothers and parents would all bow down to him one day. Joseph's ten older brothers hated him for this, and they sold him into slavery, allowing their father to believe he was killed. Joseph lived dark years as a slave in the house of Potiphar, but he served diligently. Nevertheless, Potiphar's wife lied and accused him of rape. He was imprisoned for more than a decade. Joseph spent more than twenty years either enslaved or in prison in Egypt.

But Joseph's childhood dream would come to fruition. He used his gift of dream interpretation to help Pharaoh lead Egypt out of a great famine. He was given tremendous authority, second only to Pharaoh himself. What his brothers and others had meant for evil, God meant for good and for the saving of many lives.

There is so much we can draw from Joseph's story. Like him, you've been given gifts, and you've been dealt a hand in life that may look incomprehensible. But we can better understand these gifts and how they play into God's plans.

Reading Joseph's story in Genesis, we watch him be so sure of God and his gifts—perhaps a little arrogant about it—and then we watch him face rejection and betrayal from his older brothers, who were supposed to protect him and never leave him. We watch him serve his guts out as a slave, only to be falsely accused when he was doing the right thing. We watch him sit in a prison cell for more than a decade as he continued to talk about God and trust Him.

When we've wanted to be so mad at God, Joseph's story stops us dead in our tracks. Here was a man who trusted God through suffering even though God was making no sense. Joseph was given a dream that he had no idea what to do with at first. But he was full of a hope that disarmed the very worst kinds of loneliness and suffering. He was filled with a purpose that transcended his seemingly purposeless circumstances. And at the end of a twenty-year tunnel of suffering and isolation, a light broke through. Joseph finally got to see why all of the difficulty was necessary. To those of us watching who cannot yet see relief and purpose—and perhaps won't this side of heaven—in Joseph's story we taste something bigger than pain and circumstance.

God was not far or flippant; He was strategically executing the most brilliant of plans to save lives. Our sufferings are not invisible to Him. He knows, and He will take this hell on earth and someday show us how hell was building heaven.

CHRISTINA'S STORY

Christina wrote to tell me her experience:

> I was diagnosed with stage-three breast cancer in February 2014. I was in the best shape of my life, and I was the healthiest I have ever been. I know this disease can happen to anyone. I know that in my case it would be used to do the will of God.

One night she sensed the Spirit of God telling her that there was a purpose for this disease, and that her experience would be used to help other women. It might be awful, but she was not to be afraid.

> I had been away from the Lord for quite a while at that point in my life. I was thirty-one and completely lost and feeling abandoned. But at that moment I knew that He had not abandoned me and that He loved me more than I could ever realize. I recommitted my life, and after that moment it has been amazing.

After her chemo she began the difficult process of searching for her threads with the God who had not abandoned her. Despite it all, she said:

> I feel that my entire life finally made sense for the first time. I could finally see that God had a plan, and I could see all the obstacles

that I had to go through in order to keep persevering. I finally cared about my life and my purpose for the first time.

So many can testify to a sovereign God who is loving, good, and perfect in His will—even if it looks like chaos. He makes beautiful things out of dust. So we will bring the messy threads that make us human to Him and see if He will sort them out.

I think God can untangle your soul, your story, your gifts, your people, your place, and your passions, and He can begin to weave them all into purposes that you haven't been brave enough to imagine.

DIFFICULT STUFF

We are about to transcend the realm of comfortable reading. This is going to get into your business. Even if you and I were sitting across from each other having coffee and figuring this out (which I deeply wish could be the case), a supernatural breakthrough would need to occur. Tackling the specific and intricate pieces of your life will take God plopping Himself in the middle of us and issuing discernment and revelation through black-and-white words on a page and many notes marked in a journal. This is a process. But you will come out of this different. You may even glimpse God and His grand design for your threads.

I don't know if you are sitting in a bed about to nod off, or if you are on an airplane or a beach or in a coffee shop or surrounded by little toddlers pulling on you. All journeys have a cost. The path to our purpose here is rarely built comfortably. So are you restless enough to go here? Are you hungry enough to do the work?

As you move through the remaining days, even if there are parts of this journey you do not understand, keep going.

My peace is that God is with you carrying on the good work He began in you, and oh, I pray these next few days will be just that. God revealing and speaking and moving you deeper into His love and plans for you.

Praise be to the God and Father of our Lord Jesus Christ, the Father of compassion and the God of all comfort, who comforts us in all our troubles, so that we can comfort those in any trouble with the comfort we ourselves receive from God. (2 Cor. 1:3–4)

He is with you, loving you and comforting you and leading you so that we can love and comfort and lead others to Him.

JOSEPH'S STORY

Before we begin, it would be helpful to read through Joseph's story, found in Genesis 37–50. Here is a chart of some of the major events of Joseph's life.

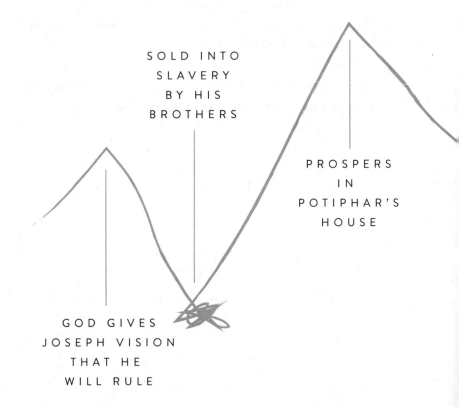

SOLD INTO
SLAVERY
BY HIS
BROTHERS

PROSPERS
IN
POTIPHAR'S
HOUSE

GOD GIVES
JOSEPH VISION
THAT HE
WILL RULE

THROWN
INTO
PRISON
IN EGYPT

MADE
RULER
IN EGYPT

READ & REFLECT

From the scriptures and story of Joseph:

Describe the journey to
Joseph's purpose.

Describe Joseph's gifts.

Describe Joseph's attitude throughout his journey.

How might he have felt in the decades of suffering?

What do you think God's perspective on Joseph's suffering was?

After reading these passages, consider the answers to these two questions:

Who are You, Lord?
What do You want for me?

GOD'S STORY, GOD'S GLORY

In the beginning God . . .

—GENESIS 1:1

My son Cooper was born and lived three and a half years of his life in Rwanda. When he was five he often wrestled with the fact that his skin color is a few—strike that—a *lot* of shades darker than his brother's and mine and Zac's and his sisters'. He kept running his hand up and down my arm and asking me, "Where can we go that I can get skin like this?" My insides fell apart.

He didn't know the painful history of his skin color in our country yet. He just wanted to be like his family. His identity is unique. He has a heritage that each of us appreciates deeply, but we do not share. So he quietly asked me as we lay in bed before prayers:

"Why did God make me born in Rwanda?"

"Why did God put me in another mommy's tummy?"

"Why did God make me?"

I can't deny that the answers to many of my son's questions are painful. Abandonment usually undergirds the beautiful tragedy of adoption, and finding himself in a loving family now can never make that painful truth go away.

It was usually dark as we lay in bed to pray and talk, and Cooper didn't know that every time he asked those questions, I had tears running down my face as I preached my guts out in his bottom bunk. And ya'll better believe I turned all charismatic preacher. Because I wanted nothing more than for Cooper to believe what I was about to say to him.

"Not one part of you is by accident. God made you and placed you in your Rwandan mama's tummy, but He knew even then that I would be your forever mama and we would be your forever family. We were made for you and you were made for us.

"Cooper, you were made to show the world God, so God gave you a special story because He has a very special purpose for you. Everything God gives you: your Rwanda, your America, your dark skin, and your strong legs; your hurts, your words, your blessings, and your smart mind—everything you have is to use for God while you are here.

"And God will show you how. Soon we will be in heaven with Him forever, and while we are here now, we get to use all we have to love people for God."

My son needed to know his life was on purpose and for a purpose. He wanted to know he wasn't an accident. I can never take away the pain of his story, but I can keep telling him there is purpose.

We all want to know we are not accidents. We all want to know our stories are going somewhere. Deep down, we are all built to live for a story bigger than ourselves—the story of the One who made us. "He has . . . set eternity in the human heart" (Eccl. 3:11).

But Cooper will never make sense of his life until he understands that eternal story and the One who made him and placed him in his spot. It's a big earth, and when he studies it, he sees countries separated by a huge ocean. He feels lost and small in it. I think a lot of us feel lost and small.

We often try to find "God's will for me" without simply first understanding God's will—God's story. But we will only discover His will for us within His will for this earth, for eternity, and for His people. We were made for this story—His story. And yes, He wrote little parts for each of us in His story. Or else we wouldn't exist.

THE ARROW

A line stretches out as far as the mind can imagine, beginning with God and with no end in sight. Think of it like the arrow we saw depicted in Joseph's story. This is the unending story of our God, who ran after us to make us His children. Each of us is like one dot in that arrow.

My Cooper, and Rahab and Oprah and Abraham Lincoln and Alexander the Great, and every other human have found their stories in the confines of God's story. The history of the world fits in a small crevice of the history of God. And throughout history, God is after one great purpose. To understand our purposes, we must remember God's ultimate agenda.

Remember: God is most after His glory. And glory is the visible expression of God's goodness and beauty on this earth. It's how we recognize Him.

Every one of our unique callings will display hints of the glory of our God. We were made to do great things, but we cannot live with motives unchecked. If our motive is the glory of God, we have tremendous freedom to dream with hearts that are completely His.

GOD'S STORY

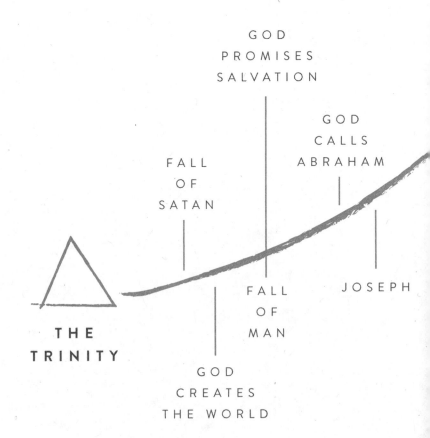

GOD
PROMISES
SALVATION

GOD
CALLS
ABRAHAM

FALL
OF
SATAN

**THE
TRINITY**

FALL
OF
MAN

JOSEPH

GOD
CREATES
THE WORLD

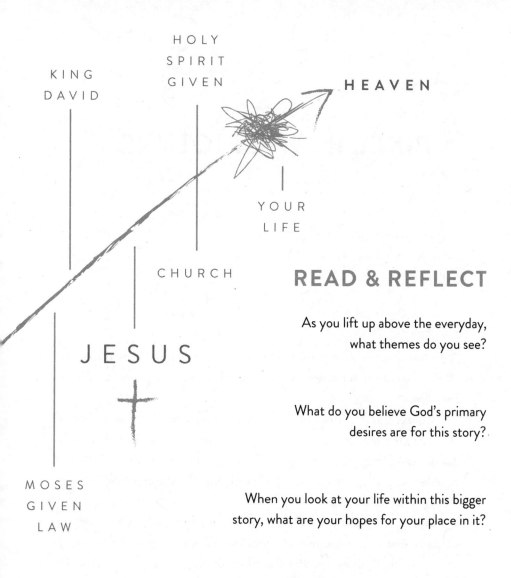

KING
DAVID

HOLY
SPIRIT
GIVEN

HEAVEN

YOUR
LIFE

CHURCH

JESUS

MOSES
GIVEN
LAW

READ & REFLECT

As you lift up above the everyday,
what themes do you see?

What do you believe God's primary
desires are for this story?

When you look at your life within this bigger
story, what are your hopes for your place in it?

As you reflect on God's story, God's glory,
consider the answers to these two questions:

Who are You, Lord?
What do You want for me?

A PIXEL IN THE PICTURE

I have come down from heaven not to do my will but to do the will of him who sent me.

—JOHN 6:38

The ultimate visible expression of God's glory on earth is Jesus. How did He live out the reflection of His Father here? Jesus followed God's will for Him.

Concerning the story of God, we have a tremendous responsibility. We are to live out the same call. God has chosen to show Himself and His goodness—His glory—through us. And like the millions of pixels that together display an image on a TV, every one of our unique callings will display God to our world.

When we finally got a flat-screen TV, my husband set it up only to discover that one of the tens of thousands of pixels was out. One dumb pixel just didn't show up, and the entire display was affected. That TV went back.

Believe me. I know it feels near ridiculous to live for things we can't yet see. At the base of our souls, each of us needs to figure out whether we are building God's glory or our own. This could be the biggest hurdle we must cross before living our purposes. No matter how magnificent your pixel here, remember we will be only one brief little light unless we are part of the bigger thing we were made for.

> Just as a body, though one, has many parts, but all its many parts form one body, so it is with Christ. . . .
>
> Now if the foot should say, "Because I am not a hand, I do not belong to the body," it would not for that reason stop being part of the body. . . .
>
> The eye cannot say to the hand, "I don't need you!" And the head cannot say to the feet, "I don't need you!" . . . so that there should be no division in the body, but that its parts should have equal concern for each other.
>
> Now you are the body of Christ, and each one of you is a part of it. (1 Cor. 12:12, 15, 21, 25, 27)

God built us uniquely, issuing different gifts and stories and places and people, then called us to move as *one*. So whether our role is to mother or start a business or sponsor a child or sweep a floor or run a bank or teach little people to read, we don't want to miss it.

His Spirit will pour us into need, and who are we to judge where and what is the greatest need? This isn't as much about what or where as it is about getting over ourselves and just doing it. I want to have a faith God can move through.

But dadgumit, I am selfish. And so are you. We won't do this perfectly. God overcomes us and our distracted rebel selves with Christ. "He is the radiance of the glory of God and the exact imprint of his nature, and he upholds the universe by the word of his power. After making purification for sins, he sat down at the right hand of the Majesty on high" (Heb. 1:3 ESV).

Christ in us is our hope for a world we can't yet see. For the joy set before Him, He endured the cross. It is a joy that we share: His joy was us, and our joy is Him. It means forever with a God who is entirely good, and who chose us in Him to become His children.

SECURE

The rudder that keeps us fixed is our identity in Christ. We leave behind a life spent proving ourselves when we find the freedom of covering our mistakes and our inadequacy with the holiness and power of our Savior. We get to run with confidence, not in ourselves but in our God.

I want Cooper to understand he isn't just made for *a* purpose; he was placed in this time and space for the *greatest imaginable* purpose. He will show God to a world that doesn't know Him—in his beautiful and unique way. He will bring light to darkness. He will assemble the pieces of his life, not into a tower for his own name that would only crumble, but for the name of the one God Almighty. That's the hope—that's my prayer—that's the sermon he's going to keep hearing.

"Faith is confidence in what we hope for and assurance about what we do not see" (Heb. 11:1). I'll be honest: I have given my life to this story, and there are still days I wonder if it is all real. It's okay if you waver sometimes. God holds us in place with Him; we don't hold ourselves. Where your faith is weak, pray and ask Him for more. My prayer is this: "I do believe; help me overcome my unbelief!" (Mark 9:24).

Help our unbelief, God. Give us faith that Your arrow never ends, and that to live as a part of it is the reason we were created. We get to be part of the story of God, and I want nothing more than to run with You, a God who would die for me.

We get to be part of giving people God.

RESPOND

"Faith is confidence in what we hope for and assurance about what we do not see" (Heb. 11:1). How confident are you that the story of God is real? Explain your answer and how it affects your life.

How confident are you that Jesus is your Savior? Explain your answer and how that confidence or absence of it affects your life.

How confident are you that God has specific purposes for you in His story? Explain. What difference has that made to you?

READ & REFLECT

> [Christ] is the radiance of the glory of God and the
> exact imprint of his nature . . .
>
> **HEBREWS 1:3** ESV

If Christ is the exact imprint of God's nature, use the following chart to
describe how Christ reacted to each thing listed, using your knowledge of
Christ's story for guidance. In the far-right column, write a few descriptive
words about what those actions tell us about God's nature.

	CHRIST'S ACTION TOWARD . . .	GOD'S NATURE
Temptation	He fought it and was victorious over it (see Mark 1:13)	persevering, holy
Religiousness		
Sinners		

	CHRIST'S ACTION TOWARD . . .	GOD'S NATURE
Sickness		
Forgiveness		
The Devil		
This life		
Heaven		
Money		

YOUR STORY

While Joseph was there in the prison, the LORD was with him.

—GENESIS 39:20–21

One night, as we wrestled through our stories together in our Austin class, Margaret leaned in to describe her passions. She adjusted her spunky, dark-rimmed glasses and described her job, which also happens to be her passion. Margaret tells the stories of people suffering around the world using the medium of film. When I asked her why she loves her work, she quickly answered, "I want people to really be heard and understood. To be seen. And I want to move those watching to be a part of healing their hurt."

She doubted that these passions were in any way connected to her own story. So we asked her to tell us her story.

She showed little emotion as she described a childhood built in a home with no parents. She was the oldest of three siblings, and their dad had abandoned their family when they were very young. Their mom was not healthy and would leave them home alone while she went to unknown places for months at a time. Their grandparents lived next door and helped some, but Margaret shouldered the burden of caring for her little brother and sister.

We were all speechless, and tears flowed as we tried to imagine a home with no parents and three children turning the lights out and locking the doors and tucking themselves in at night.

But Margaret didn't cry and issued this disclaimer: "It's not a big deal. We were okay. We always had what we needed."

I whispered the only words that I could think. "Margaret—that is not okay. I am so sorry." Then she started to cry. She had learned to be brave, not complain, work hard. If she cried, who would have comforted her anyway? We did our best to allow her tears to fall in a safe space.

Then one of Margaret's close friends said, "Can you really not see that your story has birthed your passions?" She still shook her head no, and we were in disbelief that what screamed to us was invisible to her.

"You spend your life helping invisible people to be seen. To be heard. And you move others to respond to their needs." Margaret leaned back in her chair, uncomfortable with the thought but allowing it to press in.

What if the darkest moments of your life God intended for good?

And what if the purest moments of bliss contained your greatest contributions to this world?

God speaks through story because that is how we best understand the most important things.

ARROWS POINTING

That arrow we talked about—the one we're each a dot in—is a fluid line symbolizing motion, a line that technically has no end. An arrow points to something. It leads to something. So if we are not by accident, and the events of our lives are not accidents either, then it's all leading to something. Take Joseph: he was never in the wrong place at the wrong time, though it must have felt wrong to him (prison anyone?). God was leading him through a series of events that all served great purpose. Even though it was all leading to a specific time and place, it was also building a man God could use.

Sure, our stories lead us toward our purposes, but they also make us into people strong enough to fulfill our purposes.

Margaret was no different than Joseph or any of us in her calling. She was shaped by the events of her life; she was moved toward others because of her own suffering; she was most fulfilled investing into the world the deepest needs that she had been denied. God was working for good and even for the saving of lives.

Joseph met the need in Egypt because he had . . .

- the unique gifting to meet the need;
- compassion and character that comes through suffering;
- the right people in his path;
- the gift of turning up in all the right places, even if they all felt wrong;
- and a passion to see it through.

I know your story is sacred; maybe the most sacred pieces of you lie there. I also know that memories are often more foggy than clear. And I also know that you may not see the point yet.

To build a picture of your story—the events that have shaped you—is a powerful and beautiful thing. It's the darkest and most beautiful moments lined up on an arrow. You will see things you have never seen before.

As I went through this process, I started to see something. Every painful and beautiful thing was moving me somewhere . . . the most heart-wrenching things were birthing something. I couldn't deny it.

I could look back and for the first time see that the sparks of my greatest passions were lit and fed in these moments. I didn't know exactly where they were taking me, but I could see they weren't by accident. This was a good story—possibly even a great one.

I want you to consider today that your story could be a great one. Begin by charting some points—the highlights and the sufferings—that characterize your story.

YOUR STORY

BIRTH

RESPOND

01 Identify a highlight from each life stage when you felt pleasure in what you were doing. When were moments you remember being proud and satisfied?

EXAMPLE   *painting with my grandfather*

0–6

7–12

13–18

19–24

25+

THE
PRESENT

02   Identify a memory from each life stage when you remember suffering.

EXAMPLE   *my parents divorced*

0–6

7–12

13–18

19–24

25+

03   Now lay out these moments on your arrow.

THREADS OF GIFTS

If I speak in the tongues of men or of angels, but do not have
love, I am only a resounding gong or a clanging cymbal.

—1 CORINTHIANS 13:1

Those times on our arrows when we felt most fully satisfied, those can point us to our gifts.

When we laid out our stories during our study in Austin, Jessica and Hannah pulled their chairs together to share. Jessica held the notes revealing her most sacred moments. As she looked back over the list of times when she had felt God's pleasure and felt fully satisfied, all the moments had to do with a stage. Performing in a school musical, being elected student council president, giving a talk at a leadership summit.

She realized she had to share them with Hannah, whom she barely knew. So she cynically laughed and said, "I am not sure if these moments display my gifts or my selfishness."

I had watched Jessica wrestle internally for clarity of purpose for years. Yet when that girl prays or teaches, the whole room worships. She exudes an authentic passion. And yet Jessica was terrified of herself. She is gifted—a leader, a teacher, a visionary—but she was barely using her gifts because of many distinct fears. As we sat together digging up all her fear, she boiled it down for us.

She is afraid that if she runs too fast with her strengths as a single woman, men will find her too strong—too abrasive. She is afraid of dreaming and trying and facing failure or disappointment. She is afraid of her own selfish ambition or the sin that may come out if she really pursued opportunities to use her gifts. She wonders if God made a mistake. Why would He give a woman all this strength?

That night Hannah looked at Jessica and said, "These moments that you feel so happy—performing and leading—would be my worst nightmares. Your pleasure in those moments? God has put that in you."

Jessica called me later to say, "For some reason I thought everyone craved a stage. Maybe I have a responsibility to quit being afraid of my motives and start using the gifts and passions God has put in me."

She is super analytical, and so am I, and so are a lot of you. We often overanalyze clear, simple truths. We tell ourselves it is right to be afraid. I don't know what your fears are, but I know if they aren't from God they are from the Enemy, and they need to be taken apart.

We are all unique and needed in this plan. To hide our gifts, or to deny them, or to compare and wish them away is not only taking from yourself but also taking from God, His church, and a world that needs to see the expression of God that He designed you to bring.

CREATED TO RUN

What if you have God-given gifts and He wants to turn you loose with them?

What if you were built for a fast racetrack, and you are camped out in a parking lot?

I have talked to so many people who are driving around a parking lot, and they can't figure out why they feel so discontent. But they are afraid that if they pull out onto a real racetrack,

- they wouldn't have anything to contribute.
- they would go too fast—get out of control.
- they would lose.
- they would wreck.
- people would judge them.

Joseph had a crazy dream—he probably shouldn't have rubbed a dream like that in his older brothers' faces. I picture this as a parking-lot season for him: brash and arrogant, using his God-given gift for his own purposes. He was going to change the world, and they all were going to bow down to him.

It was a good day—one you may have tasted, with rare moments of vision and clarity when you see your gifts. You have a vision but then . . . silence. Twenty years of waiting were coming for him, with no whisper of that vision. No one was bowing down. In fact, he experienced the opposite—he was dishonored, mocked, hated. In the wait, Joseph had to decide if he loved God no matter what. No matter what his story was, what his circumstances were. Was he staying in with this God?

I am beginning to think God's favorite word in the entire universe is *wait*. He doesn't use it a lot in the Bible, but we all know it's true. He loves to make us all wait. There is a season for everything, and racing fast around a track with your gifts and vision in Technicolor may not be for today. But He is working in the waiting.

There is a purpose for all of this; there is a track with side rails; there is a reason God gives us gifts. We will experience the pleasure of racing while

God is using us, but our gifts' primary purpose is building up others. This may mean a God-given season in the parking lot.

We will look at God's design for all of us to participate as different parts of one body. But there is no entitlement in it. Read what Paul said right after he told us we are each gifted uniquely:

> If I speak in the tongues of men or of angels, but do not have love, I am only a resounding gong or a clanging cymbal. If I have the gift of prophecy and can fathom all mysteries and all knowledge, and if I have a faith that can move mountains, but do not have love, I am nothing. If I give all I possess to the poor and give over my body to hardship that I may boast, but do not have love, I gain nothing. (1 Cor. 13:1–3)

It could be that our time in the parking lots of life is meant to teach us to love. There are often long, drawn-out seasons of waiting between recognizing our gifts and using them to their full potential. And there are often painfully long seasons between the glimpse of a vision and its fulfillment.

Whether you're waiting now or racing full-speed ahead, give some thought to your gifts and how they've played out in your life so far.

GIFTS

RESPOND

What was it about Joseph's story that stood out to you this week? Why?

Do you feel as though you're in a parking lot or on a racetrack? Why?

Have you ever been through a season of waiting that turned out to teach you love? Describe it.

How does 1 Corinthians 13:2 apply to your life? Have you ever witnessed or used a gift without love and felt it lacking? What was it like?

Go back in time a little. What did your parents or friends tell you that you were good at growing up?

Refer to your arrow from Day 19 as you fill out the table to the right.

YOUR MOMENTS	WHY YOU FELT SATISFIED

NATURAL ABILITIES AND SPIRITUAL GIFTS

*Every good and perfect gift is from above, coming
down from the Father of the heavenly lights.*

—JAMES 1:17

All of us have natural abilities we are born with and spiritual gifts we are given when we become believers and are filled and empowered by the Spirit.

When I was a kid, I loved directing my cousins in our homemade Christmas pageant. I remember being completely exhilarated by it: the leading and the directing, the moving people together toward a goal. At that point I had not yet seen my own need for the Savior I knew so much about. But God had already placed in me natural abilities as an expression of His creativity. It was part of His plan to someday use my little gifts and my personality and my work to display Himself to my little portion of the world.

The moment I was saved and filled with the Spirit at seventeen years old, every natural, God-given ability transformed and expanded into one new focus. God took my natural ability to lead, and I gathered younger girls and began to teach my Bible. Strike that—I preached my Bible. I had a new, supernatural gift of teaching. I had never seen it before, and it just poured out of me.

So now my natural abilities were being used supernaturally for God's purposes, and the Spirit was giving me a new gift that I could use to show His glory more fully on this earth.

Let me be clear: I can look back from where I am now and see this. At the time, I was uncertain and insecure, and I had no idea what the words *spiritual gifts* even meant. I can promise you, my gifts were wild and undeveloped—for crying out loud, I was seventeen. So before you picture magical moments, hear that this has been a lifelong journey of discovering and growing in a gifting. You may have only hints of your gifts, or maybe they are perfectly clear to you, or maybe you think you have nothing good to offer.

We are going to dig a little. We are going to get under the hood and see what is in you. What has God given you to bring Him glory here?

What are you just flat great at? Don't go all spiritual on me. Are you a great storyteller, or are you funny, or are you a musician, or are you great at math or problem-solving or listening or running?

Or are you good with your hands, all Pinterest crafty? I don't like you if you are good at that kind of stuff, but I get that you can't help it. My sister and my mom are brilliant party hosts and chefs and home-makers and designers. I fight jealousy and inadequacy as I stir powdered pink lemonade in a plastic yellow pitcher for my kind of hostessing, but whatever.

For just a moment compare yourself to no one else and lay down every picture of what you think it looks like to be gifted for God. Think about what you love and what you are great at. If you are a believer in Jesus, this may be how God's Spirit has gifted you to build up His church.

THE PLEASURE OF GOD

Eric Liddell was born in 1902, the son of missionaries in China. His story is retold in the film *Chariots of Fire*. Eric felt called to give his life to God, and in that pursuit he trained and planned to become a missionary like his parents. But Eric had a gift. He could run, and every door was opening for him to do it. Doors opened all the way to the Olympics. As the film portrays Eric processing his calling and his gifts with his sister, he says these famous words: "I believe God made me for a purpose, but he also made me fast. And when I run I feel his pleasure."[1]

Some of us are hung up on looking for super-spiritual gifts like prophecy or healing. But what if you are just fast? What if you are a great musician? What if you excel at accounting? What if you feel God's pleasure as you design buildings or format PTA calendars?

When do you feel God's pleasure?

The answer to this question will help you determine the unique things He has given you. There is no spiritual and secular divide; we built those divisions. "Whatever you do, do it all for the glory of God" (1 Cor. 10:31). Even the seemingly small and boring parts that may not seem spiritual.

We are all given things so that we might show God to others. The raw materials of our lives will come together and be used to bless others and build God's kingdom.

INVENTORY

Here are just a few examples of gifts mentioned throughout Scripture. These are just to get you thinking. Some might jump right out at you and say, "This is you!" Others you might not be sure of. If you would like to delve into spiritual gifts further, see each word's exact meaning and discover which ones fit you. Plenty of resources and Bible commentaries can take you down that road, including many online spiritual gifts tests.[2]

In addition to 1 Corinthians 12, other great passages for further study of gifts are:

- Romans 12
- Ephesians 4
- 1 Peter 4

Once you've had some time to think, circle the gifts that you have seen God use in your life in the past.

Prophecy // Teaching // Exhortation // Encouragement // Service // Giving // Leadership // Mercy // Apostleship // Wisdom // Knowledge // Faith // Miracles // Healing // Administration // Discernment // Evangelism // Pastoring // Shepherding // Hospitality // Missions

Describe two or three times you remember God using these circled gifts through you.

REMEMBER

Sometimes the greatest perspective on our giftings comes from processing this with other people. With Day 20's table in hand, sit down with a friend or roommate or family member and discuss these questions and your memories. You can do this over the phone or over coffee. Here are some questions to ask.

When have you seen me operating in my sweet spot?

What do you think I do well?

In what ways have you seen me grow and develop my gifts in the last few years?

Have I helped you grow? If so, how?

As you look through my moments, what stands out to you?

RESPOND

Make a list of the things you are great at.

When do you feel God's pleasure?

In light of this and the projects you've just completed, compare the list of things you're good at, the spiritual gifts you may have, and the places you feel God's pleasure. Where do you see overlap?

Do you think any of your natural abilities are becoming spiritual gifts? Or have they in the past? In what ways could these things be God's Spirit gifting you to build up His church?

When you look at your list of gifts and "raw materials," what excites you? What are you grateful for?

THREADS OF SUFFERING

We boast in the hope of the glory of God. Not only so, but we also glory in our sufferings, because we know that suffering produces perseverance; perseverance, character; and character, hope.

—ROMANS 5:2–4

Out of our pain we will heal our world. This isn't a trite saying; it is truth. Because whatever we failed to receive as children, we most want to give. So we don't dig up the past without just cause. We dig up the past because it is some of the most fertile material in our lives.

A lot of my friends have compost piles. If you don't know what that is, just picture a pile of rotting food in the corner of your suburban backyard. Any waste in your home that can decompose you put out there: banana peels, pizza crusts, coffee grounds. If you are really lucky, you have a pet who contributes his waste. Okay, clear enough.

Most everyone accompanies their compost pile with a lovely, frugal little vegetable garden. Their compost is the most fertile soil; Miracle-Gro can't compete with this stuff, so they say.

The messiest waste of our lives becomes the most fertile soil.

———

My childhood family was the idyllic picture of my parents' generation of the American dream. My parents were involved socially and at church, and they were raising three girls who behaved and appeared to love God. My dad tucked us in every night on his knees and prayed for us beside our beds. But somehow, amid all the good, I grew up feeling like I could never reach an invisible moving mark, and it haunted me. The pain of that chased me into adulthood and seemed to grow, not fade.

Approval was oxygen, and many times it felt as if I could not breathe. This particular ache, this chase, contained my greatest fear and my greatest pursuit.

Years later my dad would apologize for the hurts this caused in my childhood. He shared about the hurts from his own childhood full of similar pressure and inadequacy. Our struggles almost always take root in our childhoods, and those struggles can go on to entangle us for our entire lives. Or, if we are brave enough to face them, they could be the greatest weapons we have to help set others free.

The deep holes I was working to fill would eventually define what I would most desire to give away to the world.

What are your holes?

In the very best of stories there is a moment that is so dark you are unsure how the characters or your own soul will ever recover. *Braveheart*, *Titanic*, even *Peter Pan*. You can't see the road out when everyone is tied up and about to die. Very few cruel stories ever leave you there, but the best of stories always go there.

CHANGED OR CRUSHED

Everyone reading this has tasted some version of suffering. We live in a broken world, and it's just overflowing with it. We're all tempted to shut down when the fire gets too hot. But we can do one of two things with suffering: we can absorb it and let it change us, or we can let it crush us.

Suffering will change you, or it will crush you.

I know people to whom it's done both. Honestly, on a given day it does both to me at the same time. We're building the stories of our lives—the highest points and the lowest points. Something about the highest points reveals what it is we were made to do that brings God pleasure.

But it is trickier to consider that God knew about every single darkness that you would face before you ever faced it. Every single one. He knew it. I don't say that lightly or without a lot of fear and trembling because I know some of you are dealing with unthinkable hurt.

GOD HIDES HERE

God didn't let Joseph just be sold into slavery so he could get to Egypt; He had Joseph's brothers do it. He could have found another way. But God absolutely devastated Joseph. For twenty years, the only people who had really known him before he was a nameless slave wanted him dead.

So Joseph was stuck in a life of slavery and prison, and outside of that life there was no hope of an earthly family who loved him. A person in prison who has no one on the outside—not one other person on earth who cares if he is alive . . . What does that force someone to do?

Often that person cries out to God and seeks to know Him. When you don't have anything or anyone else on earth, all of a sudden God starts looking really good. Something about us needs to long for heaven. When everything is right and everything works, be honest—we don't long for heaven or for God. We just don't.

We live differently when we are crushed. Arrogance is born when there is no crushing. We need to want Jesus. God knows that. There is not one part of you that He dismisses. There is not one tear you will ever cry that is not felt deeply by God. But He is not afraid to let us suffer. We can't get away from it.

Paul said, "We boast in the hope of the glory of God. Not only so, but we also glory in our sufferings, because we know that suffering produces perseverance; perseverance, character; and character, hope" (Rom. 5:2–4).

Before we get bitter and ask how this could happen, how God could ever say that unimaginable suffering is worth it, look what Paul made clear in the next verses:

> And hope does not put us to shame, because God's love has been poured out into our hearts through the Holy Spirit, who has been given to us. You see, at just the right time, when we were still powerless, Christ died for the ungodly. Very rarely will anyone die for a righteous person, though for a good person someone might possibly dare to die. But God demonstrates his own love for us in this: While we were still sinners, Christ died for us. (Rom. 5:5–8)

Paul quickly warns us not to question God's love because God chose the worst kind of suffering because of His love for us. As we begin to process our suffering, remember: you have a Savior who not only understands suffering but who saved you through it and will use it to build a beautiful story. While any number of feelings may wash over you as you recall your suffering, let that truth be your anchor.

RESPOND

In the chart below, for each life stage identify a time you remember suffering. Do not overthink it. Just write down the first things that come to mind in the "Memory" column.

Here are some questions to get you thinking. (Some of you will have no problem remembering the most painful moments of your life. I am so sorry.)

Did anyone hurt you?

What circumstances were out of your control?

When did you feel afraid?

When do you remember crying?

Next, go back and write a couple of descriptive words to answer the question, "What specifically about that moment was most hurtful to you?"

	MEMORY	WHAT HURT
example	my parents divorced	insecure about future
0–6		
7–12		
13–18		
19–24		
25+		

CONSIDER

It is difficult for us to consider God's purposes for our suffering if we are still walking around with gaping, open wounds. Are they scars yet? Or still bleeding? When you look back at these moments, is there still a lot of pain in remembering? I am a big believer in Christian counseling, and that may be an important step in your healing, but no study or book or counselor can do what Jesus can do. He suffered and wants to walk with you through your suffering as the open wounds heal into scars, leaving a memory and a mark but losing their sting.

As you process your dark moments, write a letter to Jesus. If you are angry or sad, that is okay. Be honest and tell Him your thoughts on these moments.

_____

_____

_____

_____

_____

_____

_____

_____

_____

_____

READ & REFLECT

I want to be sensitive to your processing. This step may not be appropriate yet. If you just wrote down things you have never shared with anyone, or if you are still deeply grieving a loss or abuse, this step may be too difficult right now. So I am giving you permission to lay it down, whether for months or years, and seek healing from God, with the help you need from others.

If you are ready to move forward, devote some time to figuring out how you can best interact with these questions. Some of you are verbal processors, and others are internal processors. You can take this step by yourself or with family or with a friend.

Below, rewrite a list of each moment you shared. Then beside it write how that moment has played a part in shaping you.

Write some possible ways God could use each experience to help someone else.

WHY DO WE SUFFER?

You intended to harm me, but God intended it for good to accomplish what is now being done, the saving of many lives.

—GENESIS 50:20

We still come back to the question, why does God let us suffer?

Jesus is best known through suffering. Every time I want to be mad at God because of suffering, He shows me Jesus. As the Bible puts it, "I want to know Christ—yes, to know the power of his resurrection and participation in his sufferings" (Phil. 3:10). And it is true: I have known Jesus most deeply in suffering. He seems to inhabit suffering, and He endured it too. He is not a God unfamiliar with suffering, and He is near our broken hearts.

WHEN WE SUFFER

We get stronger. With suffering comes a morbid but helpful perspective that life is moving fast and this earth is not our home. I used to live in fear that my life wasn't going to work out just right. The more I surrender to suffering, and to joy, and to whatever God has for me, the less I worry about that. Now my biggest fear is that I won't spend my life well for God.

I can run further and longer than I could before. I am not despairing; faith is growing.

We hurt for heaven. I remember a day when we sat at a funeral for a friend who committed suicide. The day before, the state of Oklahoma nearly blew away in tornados. It was one of those days you just hurt for heaven. After twenty-four hours of scenes of flattened neighborhoods and missing children, the whole country was hurting for all the wrongs to be made right and all the shock to be made peaceful.

Suffering often jars us out of comatose lives. As I listened to the pastor describe the life of our friend, I ached to be with him in heaven, and I also ached to live this short life with as much passion and love as humanly possible.

Suffering reminds us this life is short, and this earth is not our home. God's glory will be revealed, and those who have suffered most will be the most overjoyed.

Our lives could leave a mark. If we are here for just a breath, I'd like my one little breath to feel more like a mighty gust of wind. That takes surrender, perseverance, and not wasting my minutes away on comparing or complaining. The apostles walked away from painful persecution, "rejoicing because they had been counted worthy of suffering" (Acts 5:41).

It is an honor to suffer. It is a privilege. And we are not to waste it. God wrote suffering into our stories and wants to redeem it for His glory. And if we weren't shaking our fists at Him, we could possibly sit down and see that we are running from a life in flames toward a great purpose—a purpose that could never exist without the flames.

God promises throughout Scripture to redeem your suffering, to make beautiful things out of ashes. Nobody else can do that. He can. He can turn dead and dry bones into living life, redeem death and make it alive. He can take the most awful, horrific, terrible circumstances and bring life into them.

How will He do that?

I'll tell you how He has done it in my life.

My dad is better than ever now at telling me how proud he is of me. Looking back, I realize he has always been proud of me. Because of his own scars, he just didn't know exactly how to show me.

But as a child I could perceive only that my worst fear was coming true. The thing my soul craved more than any other was out of my reach . . . my daddy's approval.

And like all bondage, my quest for my dad's approval turned into something bigger: pleasing anyone I could. I was motivated, but the motive of my heart, the song I sang in my head, my thoughts, the way I interacted with people, what I thought about when I woke and when I lay down—they were all about trying to please people around me. I was completely chained up.

God used something dark to break chains in me and to set me free. I stood staring my worst fear in the face, and God never felt closer.

GLORIA'S STORY

Gloria wrote to me about one of the darkest times imaginable:

On December 20, 2016, a good friend of mine's baby passed away from SIDS. He was at a basketball game the night before, smiling and cooing, and gone the next day. It was devastating for so many.

In January, God kept laying on Gloria's heart to host a church Bible study in her home. Initially she resisted the commitment. But when she reached out to her good friend, Elisha, who had lost her baby, Elisha agreed to come to a home study on *Restless*. Nine women who hadn't known one another all that well connected and went deep.

When they got to the part on suffering, Gloria recalled:

Week one, Elisha talked a little. Week two, she was angry at our pastor because he said, "Elisha, I know you don't see this, but God is going to use this for His glory. Something good is going to happen." Elisha was mad because she didn't want it to be her story of a baby dying. We all shed lots of tears with her, especially on the chapter of suffering. We realized we all had experienced suffering in different ways.

By the end of their time together, Elisha shared her dream of creating a foundation in her son's name, the Knox Blocks Foundation. Its mission was to give away Owlet baby monitors, which attach to a baby's foot and monitor heartbeat and breathing on a phone app. Their goal is to save lives, and Gloria is sure that God is working miracles and saving others through the unspeakable pain she experienced when her greatest fear came true.

If our worst fears come true . . . God. And as we suffer and He comforts us, we comfort others.

INTENDED FOR GOOD

Second Corinthians 1:3–4 says, "Praise be to the God and Father of our Lord Jesus Christ, the Father of compassion and the God of all comfort, who comforts us in all our troubles, so that we can comfort those in any trouble with the comfort we ourselves receive from God."

Everywhere I go, I see people stuck in bondage to something invisible, and I lose sleep, pound the table, and spend endless hours fighting for their freedom through writing and teaching. Out of my pain I see others' pain, and because I have tasted freedom, I crave others' freedom.

- abortion recovery groups
- words penned on how to walk through a divorce you never wanted
- crying with your friend who just lost her mother
- a friend sharing for the first time that she was abused because you just shared your abuse
- moving toward caring for the fatherless through adoption because you never had a father

Out of our pain we heal. Out of our bondage we set free. And, again, the messiest waste of our lives becomes the most fertile soil.

I'm getting there, in embracing suffering. But as I embrace it, the pain seems only to increase. It helps me to read Genesis 50, where Joseph faced his brothers who had caused decades of suffering to him and said, "You intended to harm me, but God meant it for good." Then he said, "To accomplish . . . the saving of many lives" (v. 20).

Our suffering could possibly save lives. If God's arrow really does go on forever and ever and never ends, it's justifiable that God cares more about our eternity with Him than this little pixel today.

What men meant for evil, God meant for good, for the saving of many. Fires are lit in our lives, and they can burn to shine light or cause destruction. We get to decide which purpose they will serve.

RESPOND

Genesis 50:20 says, "You intended to harm me, but God intended it for good to accomplish what is now being done, the saving of many lives." Do you believe this about the suffering in your life? Can God use it for good?

Are you surprised that part of finding our purpose could be through our suffering? Is that hard for you to embrace, or do you agree?

Do you see any convictions or passions emerge when you look back at the trials you have suffered?

Second Corinthians 1:4 says that He comforts us in our troubles. How have you seen this verse play out?

Tell a short story from your own life or from someone you know about how ministry is birthed from suffering.

What is your hope as you process the suffering in your life?

Read Genesis 37:12–36 and Genesis 39.

Describe Joseph's sufferings as he might if he were plotting them on an arrow.

What stood out to you in Joseph's life and sufferings? About his attitude? About God's control in his life?

READ & REFLECT

Turn to the previous day's work, look back at your dark moments again, choose one word to represent each event, and chart each moment on the arrow below.

We will continue to work with this arrow as we move forward.

Now, reflecting on all the scriptures and what you learned from family and friends, begin to narrow down three to five passions that have been born from these dark places.

_____ | _____ | _____
_____ | _____ | _____
_____ | _____ | _____
_____ | _____ | _____

> We often long to give to the world what we failed to receive growing up.

THREADS OF PLACES

The LORD was with Joseph so that he prospered, and he lived in the house of his Egyptian master.

—GENESIS 39:2

Place is so important to our purpose; it determines the environment that nourishes us and the people we come into contact with. Our gifts are perfectly suited for a place in time. So what about your place? There is no escaping this question if we are going to look at purpose: Do we stay in our place, or do we need to go?

Some of you have jobs you hate and will be called to stay, and some of you have jobs you love and God will call you to go. The paradigm of a believer is holistically different than that of a person without God. Without a living God, you get to be your own god. With a living God who works for eternal purposes, He gets to use us however He pleases.

BE THERE

Let's start with what we can know. Our mission is to know God and make Him known. We understand at least a glimpse of the story of God through Scripture. We know we are to love, without warrant, every person God puts in our paths. And we are to love God more than anything.

You'll remember that though we may not know God's specific, detailed will for us, 99 percent of being in the will of God is being wholly *willing* to be in the will of God. He is quiet and completely wise in His timing of revealing His will.

Most of you reading this have enough opportunity for ministry right under your noses, for which you never need to move or change a thing. In Austin there is a bumper sticker floating around that says, "Life is too short to live in Dallas." Austinites think it's funny. Here is my version for our purposes today: Life is too short to spend much time worrying about where on this planet you should be. As Jim Elliott, the great missionary-then-martyr said, "Wherever you are, be all there."[1]

We live in a space in history where job changes, moves, and relocations are within reason and perfectly acceptable. So rather than be paralyzed with fear that you may move when you should have stayed or you may stay when you should have moved, pray and commit your ways to the Lord. And then go *do something*.

God asks us into His will like a loving dad in a swimming pool asking his little child to jump. Whether that child jumps really far or barely scoots on his bottom into the pool, that dad will move to catch him. So don't be afraid. God's will is moving, and if we will just jump, His will is going to catch us. Let Him be God; move on with what you know and quit over-analyzing what you don't.

Do not be anxious about anything, but in everything, by prayer and petition, with thanksgiving, present your requests to God. And the peace of God, which transcends all understanding, will guard your hearts and your minds in Christ Jesus. (Phil. 4:6–7)

Joseph did this so beautifully. God had shown him that he would do awesome things, and rather than worry about being stuck in prison or as a slave in Potiphar's house, Joseph did great things wherever he was.

Do great works wherever you are. Likewise, do not be afraid to go or afraid to stay.

We line up lives in order of splendor or impact or performance, but God is after His glory. In heaven, even the most adventurous missionaries among us won't be rewarded because of their location on earth; they will be rewarded for their obedience and faithfulness. And those who spent most of their lives in cubicles and driving Suburbans in carpool lines will be standing beside them receiving similar crowns.

It's not our place; it's what we do in our places.

———

Joseph had a determination that is missing in our generation. Not to put too fine a point on it, but I think we are a bunch of wimps. In general, we try our best to avoid difficult work. But when Joseph was in slavery and in prison, he picked up the mop and said, "Okay, I'm going to work with this. I'm going to make the best of this." That's powerful.

With no explanation from God as to why his life was in ruin, he made a choice to be a kick-butt slave. He was awesome. He gave his life to it, without any entitlement, without any complaining. He did so well that he was first promoted to running his owner's home and later to leading the prison.

For Joseph, his fulfillment took determination and a conscious choice. He gave everything he had to serve well, even as a slave and a falsely accused inmate. So if we know that no place, no job, no marriage, no child is going to perfectly fulfill us, we can choose to quit fighting for happiness and start fighting for God's glory.

It takes a determination every day to trust Him while you're still in your place.

PLACES

Name your places in the circles. For example: work,
school, neighborhood, dorm, social media.

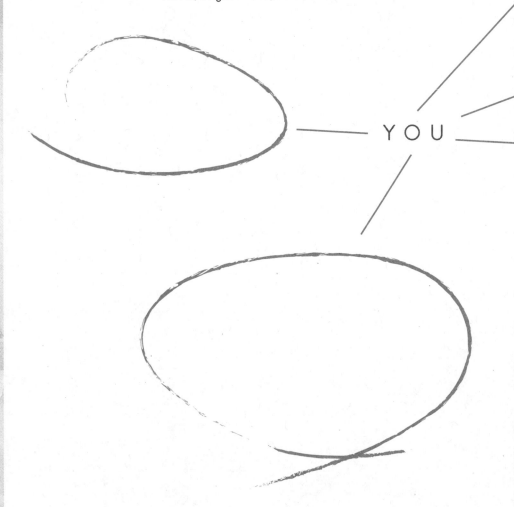

YOU

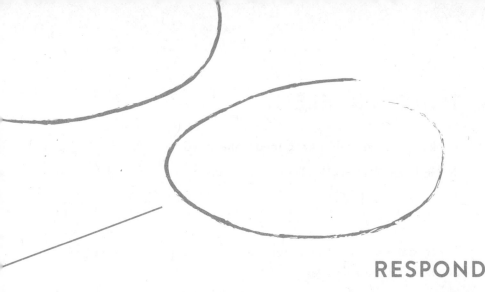

RESPOND

Lay each place before God. How might He be
moving you to act within or outside of these places?
How can you be more open to His leading?

From what you have studied this week, what is true
about your places? Do they feel insignificant? How
could you leverage your gifts or scars in these places?

"Move in what you know and quit overanalyzing what you
don't." How could these words apply to your life in your places?

What is your view of work and how is it shaped by culture?
How does it need to change to align with God's view?

READ & REFLECT

Look back at Genesis 39 and read Genesis 40.

Name Joseph's "places" in Genesis 39 and 40.

Describe the amount of control Joseph had over his circumstances (jobs and home) in these decades of his life.

In the description of the time when Joseph was enslaved and then in prison, describe what you see about his . . .

- work ethic
- concern for people
- attitude toward God
- use of his gifts
- view of waiting

Study the initiative Joseph takes in these settings. What do you learn as you watch him take initiative?

JUMPING INTO PLACE

Do not be anxious about anything, but in everything, by prayer
and petition, with thanksgiving, present your requests to God.
And the peace of God, which transcends all understanding,
will guard your hearts and your minds in Christ Jesus.

—PHILIPPIANS 4:6–7

The way we live in our places is changing the people we encounter there. Why don't we see that in our jobs, our blogs, our neighborhoods, or even our time in hospitals or infertility clinics? Often we applaud exceptional ministry and miss the everyday ministry, in everyday places, that nobody sees.

Consider: Could you be set in the places you are in because that is the most strategic place for you to preach the gospel? Let me tell you what happens when you start to think that way. Everything changes.

You change the question from "Are my neighborhood, my workplace, my school, and my life stage making me happy?" to "Are my neighborhood, my workplace, my school, and my life stage the most strategic places for my kids, my life, my story, my personality, and everything I need to preach the gospel?"

I have watched some of you come to a good answer to the first question because you quit asking it and simply considered the bigger question.

Ashley wrote to tell me about how God revealed to her the bigger question in a place that she didn't necessarily want to be. Four years ago she reluctantly sat in a room with twenty women, going through the process of identifying their threads together and dreaming about what they might mean for God. She wrote:

> I hashed out my childhood bents and began to see how God designed me. I realized I had all these gifts, but throughout the years they had just been used for selfish gain. The heart questions cut deep, exposing the motives of who I was truly living for. Myself. So with a surrendered heart I began to ask God what He would want me to do with my life. Before I knew it, this flood rushed through my soul of ache and passion for gathering women. *Gather women? How Lord? And who?* Then came the love for my city, Albuquerque.
>
> I had spent the majority of my twenties trying to escape New Mexico, and besides the weather and green chili, there are way more reasons to despise Albuquerque than to love it. It's a dark place winning awards for most homicides and worst public schools in the nation. But this new beauty began emerging from it, with a new perspective. Hope.

Soon after that small study, Ashley and her mom found themselves organizing and leading an IF:Gathering simulcast for eighty women in her town. She felt God move in her place and got a taste of what God was doing in their city. Year by year these gatherings grew to three hundred women, with multiple church partnerships. Now she serves as a women's discipleship director at her church, and she's amazed by how God brought her to where she is—in that town she'd wanted to give up on. He's gathering women, through her, in a place she had tried so hard to escape. He's changed her heart, and made her place beautiful to her—and He's showing His glory to the women around her.

Your place is not an accident; it is by design.

There are no accidents or coincidences. There is a God setting us in our times and our places with our people. And if that is true, He has a plan for it all.

I shudder to think how accidental we believe life is.

I remember talking with a girl who wept because she wanted a life of purpose. I asked what she did for a living, and she told me she was developing a sex-education program that might be used in all of the Texas school districts. *Um* . . . I was confused. How could she not feel purpose in that God-given place? She went on to realize there was incredible purpose, but she was living in so much fear that she might fail at this huge task that she couldn't embrace it.

Maybe you are exactly in the will of God, living a life of purpose, but you can't even see it because you are afraid.

Afraid your place doesn't matter.

Afraid you won't succeed.

Afraid God doesn't see you.

Afraid that what you're doing isn't ministry.

Afraid of what people will think if you live for Christ in your place.

OUR REAL PLACES

Mary embraced me the moment we met in our mutual friend's home. She sat me down and held both of my hands, eager to tell me her story and how it intersected with mine. Mary is my mom's age and recently moved with her new husband out to his country home on the outskirts of Austin. Mary insisted on meeting every neighbor, even though houses sat acres apart. But as years went by, it started to seem like so much trouble to walk all that way, and potentially creepy to drive up to their front doors.

But as she prayed a prayer of surrender, she knew God was telling her to take Him to her spread-out country neighborhood. So she decided to host a Bible study and wrote individual, handwritten letters to each neighbor inviting them to come. Immediately she gathered fifteen women who were hungry for connection, and more than a year later they are still meeting and studying the Bible.

Our places are not an accident. Your gifts and stories will be used in many different places over your lifetime. We have freedom to dream about our places; there is great purpose in using our gifts in corporations, nonprofits, state school systems, churches, and neighborhoods. Our God does not separate secular and spiritual. He just wants you to participate in His story wherever you are and with whatever you have.

If we each played our part, from Rwanda to Albuquerque, we would get to heaven and know that in our little place, we were a part of something.

I think some of you could be happy in your place if you thought that, to some degree, God was proud of you right in the midst of your mundane, punching-numbers job. We all have threads He wants to spin into stories that last forever, and our places are part of that.

Because, you know, we aren't really in our true place yet. The place we were made for is coming; no place feels quite right until we are home.

VISION

Write your places in the left-hand column of the graph below. Pray about your places, asking for wisdom, guidance, and vision.

After praying and giving it some thought, fill in the next column with a possible vision for each place. How might God want you to be intentional like Joseph in each place?

YOUR PLACES	A VISION
_____	_____
	_____
_____	_____
	_____
_____	_____
	_____
_____	_____
	_____
_____	_____
	_____

DREAM

Are you feeling free or moved to change any of your places? It's okay to consider that possibility every once in a while. Every year, Zac and I pray and ask God if we are where He wants us to be. Are our kids in the right places? Are we called to move or change anything? It keeps our hands open and allows God to move us if He wills.

So lay your places before God, writing a prayer below each one. (If you are married, include your spouse in this.)

City

Neighborhood

Jobs

Schools

Other places

How does your view of our eternal home change your view of your current one?

THREADS OF PEOPLE

Since we are surrounded by such a great cloud of witnesses, let us
throw off everything that hinders and the sin that so easily entangles.
And let us run with perseverance the race marked out for us.

—HEBREWS 12:1

Every one of us has people in our lives whom we need and people who need us. Are we intentionally spending our time in those two categories? Or are we casually bumping up against each other with no real purpose to receive or give love?

If we are honest, it is costly to love people. It is easier to survive this life on the surface, brushing up against people gently, rather than doing the mess of intentionally loving them. Love takes risk. Love takes forgiveness and grace. Love takes effort, time, and commitment. You commit not to bolt when it gets hard—because it will get hard.

And if this is the cost of deep relationship, we just don't have capacity and space to go deep with everyone. So we have to become intentional.

RUNNING PARTNERS

We have talked about the verses in Hebrews 12 that call our lives a race. We forget sometimes that how we run this race matters. So we need people who will put their fingers under our chins and lift our heads. I need that perspective in my race. I get tired and want to quit. I need people ahead of me, shouting back that it is worth it. I need deep, kindred souls beside me, making the run more fun and helping me not to feel crazy and alone.

But what's the problem with people?

They all are jacked up. Let me rephrase: *we* all are jacked up. We hurt one another. We let one another down. We disagree. I don't know if a single person with whom I am genuinely close has avoided hurting me. And I guarantee, every person who feels genuinely close to me has been hurt by me too. We are human and flawed—even those who know God.

Accepting that fact allows me to have grace for every other person who comes into my life. If I can accept that I am so broken that I am likely to hurt anyone close to me on any given day without even being aware of it, I can willingly pass out grace to those who hurt me. Zac and I save money for our children's counseling, knowing we will mess them up. As a nice gesture, we'll pay for their recovery and show up and apologize when they're eighteen. Because we know we are not perfect parents. We're not a perfect pastor and pastor's wife. We know we're not the best of friends to people. We know that we will fail people over and over again.

If I can see that I am completely messed up and that God rescued and saved me from myself, and not because I did anything or deserved it, then there is freedom in my life to issue that same grace to everybody else. I am a rescued mess of a human, and so are you. And we will hurt one another sometimes because that is what jacked-up humans do. But I still need you.

We keep running together even though we hurt one another. We must run imperfectly together. Not because we're fast or great at this or because it's always going to work out with a glorious win. But because we are committed to one another.

Here is the thing about Joseph. He stuck it out with his awful people. He committed to them, not because they were good to him but because they were his people. His brothers stabbed him in the back, selling him into two decades of slavery and prison, and they ended up standing before him in need. He didn't just give them what they needed; he gave them everything they could ever want. They were his people and he was all in, no matter what.

> Joseph said to his brothers, "I am Joseph! Is my father still living?" But his brothers were not able to answer him, because they were terrified at his presence.
>
> Then Joseph said to his brothers, "Come close to me." When they had done so, he said, "I am your brother Joseph, the one you sold into Egypt! And now, do not be distressed and do not be angry with yourselves for selling me here, because it was to save lives that God sent me ahead of you. . . ."
>
> Pharaoh said to Joseph, "Tell your brothers, 'Do this: Load your animals and return to the land of Canaan, and bring your father and your families back to me. I will give you the best of the land of Egypt and you can enjoy the fat of the land . . .'"
>
> Joseph gave them carts, as Pharaoh had commanded, and he also gave them provisions for their journey. To each of them he gave new clothing. (Gen. 45:3–5, 17–18, 21–22)

Joseph could not control his circumstances, but he intentionally leveraged every relationship in his path for the glory of God. He never wasted an opportunity to serve, even those who wronged him.

We have to pick our people and commit to them, expecting they will hurt us but not giving up easily on them when they do.

PEOPLE

Whom do you need? Who are your mission-minded, like-minded friends? Who are the people who make you love God more? Who can you safely share your soul with?

Who are wiser mentors you could pursue?

Do you believe that the people, events, and places in your life are orchestrated by God, or are they accidental? Talk about it.

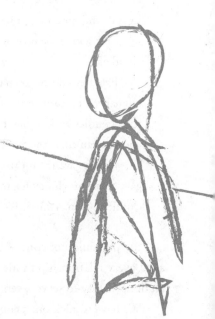

Is it difficult for you to move past small talk with people? Why?

What is God showing you in this story?

PEOPLE YOU NEED

Mentors

Friends

Family

Other

PEOPLE WHO NEED YOU

Neighbors

Coworkers

Friends

Family

Outside of acquaintances:
imprisoned, elderly, poor

Other

DAY 27

PURSUE THEM

*'Love the Lord your God with all your heart and with all your soul
and with all your mind and with all your strength.' . . . Love your
neighbor as yourself.' There is no commandment greater than these.*

—MARK 12:30–31

We don't just need people; we need the right people. Sometimes finding the right people takes discipline and effort. And then when we find them, we have to fight for them. We have to prioritize time and issue grace over and over because even the best human on this earth will disappoint us. And when that happens, you love and fight for that person even harder.

If any part of you listening to these words right now thinks to yourself, *I don't know if I have enough of the right people in my life*, you probably don't.

We all fell in love with shows like *Friends* because we deeply want to have "our people." Close friends and mentors don't fall in our laps. You search and invest, and then you allow them to be imperfect versions of what you were hoping for in your head. Most of us are waiting to be invited, waiting to be pursued, waiting for friends to come to us. But that's not the way it happens. Instead, the Bible says:

Put on then, as God's chosen ones, holy and beloved, compassionate hearts, kindness, humility, meekness, and patience, bearing with one another and, if one has a complaint against another, forgiving each other; as the Lord has forgiven you, so you also must forgive. And above all these put on love, which binds everything together in perfect harmony. And let the peace of Christ rule in your hearts, to which indeed you were called in one body. And be thankful. (Col. 3:12–15 ESV)

Love is an active process, and we are fairly lazy. So initiate. Then, when you come together, initiate depth. Great conversations come from great questions and honest answers. One of the ways I grow and experience God is over queso and salsa with kindred friends talking about deep things. It takes initiative to ask deeper questions and sheer bravery to give sincere answers. Pray and find ways to take your friendships to a deeper level.

KATE'S STORY

Kate and Ashley met when their babies became friends at daycare. From friendly hellos in the hallway at drop-off, to play-dates, to eventual dinners with their husbands in tow, they built step-by-step until they felt the shift from acquaintances to friends. Then Kate had to move. She wrote to me.

> While it would have been easy—and without a question more like me—to have hugged goodbye and chalked this relationship up as a situational friendship, there was something brewing that I believe neither one of us expected, but was absolutely God's handiwork.

Living in different communities, Kate and Ashley kept their friendship growing. They planned summer meetings and rainy family weekends and chatted on the phone on some nights. If they had ever been tempted to keep their friendship at a fun surface level, she says,

> God had other plans to use these times together to know each other's hearts better and to call each other up in how God created us and what exactly that meant for our time here on earth. Which leads me to today and writing you to share this story of friendship. Over the course of our last two years as friends, it's become more clear to us that our friendship is not happenstance. God placed Ashley and me into each other's lives for a purpose and then gave us the time and space to build on what those two sweet one-year-olds started years ago. As of late, we've been asking ourselves what, if anything, changes since we know that God orchestrated this friendship on purpose? How do we dig in deeper, especially at a distance? How do we build each other up, hold each other accountable and grow in our love for God?

Their journey led them to the process you're going through now, taking the threads of their hearts and offering them to God. Then they started leading other women through the process.

Whatever they end up doing, Kate says,

> We pray for wide-open eyes and available ears for what God has planned to do next through us—individually and together. That may mean to simply disciple one another as we have or something beyond. But regardless we pray for a willingness to go where God intends us to go.

That's the beauty of intentional friendship.

WHO NEEDS YOU?

God is after the people around you, and He pursues them through you.

I know your life may feel random and disconnected, but you cannot hear Joseph's story and tell me God didn't orchestrate the good and the bad to intersect. And you also can't tell me He would plan the details of Joseph's life and ignore yours.

Next time you are in a public space, be awkward and look in people's eyes. People—nearly every one of them—are hurting even if they don't say it. And we hold a measure of their cure. We get to give God away for our joy. I am never more content than when I am meeting needs.

Joseph looked at his brothers and said essentially, "What you meant as harm, God meant for the saving of many lives." Even after all they did to him, he thought the suffering was worth it to save people.

At some point we have to decide whether or not it is worth it to spend our lives helping people be free from bondage, meeting their needs, cheering for them as they run, giving them God. And at some point, if I find myself being completely mocked and rejected and hurt, is it still worth it for me? That is the question we all have to ask. Is it worth the saving of many lives to you?

So who needs God around you?

Pray.
Pursue them.
Ask them great questions.
Share your struggles and your God.
Dream of ways you can meet their needs.

Seek out relationships with people outside of your circles. Some of my favorite moments have happened as I stepped out of my comfort zone.

Like taking women from a local halfway house out to bowl with some of my friends. I remember sitting at a bowling alley with a woman just out of prison, who exuded more joy than I remember ever feeling in my life. She was about to see her kids, and it had been years. Her joy and perspective changed me—and I need to be changed. God's economy makes beautiful exchanges: as we give, we grow.

Seek risks and uncomfortable things. You do not risk like a fool; you are wisely investing in the only two things that will not die: God and people's souls.

Quit waiting for people to pursue you. They won't. Pursue them. Don't waste time trying to control your circumstances. Invest your time in strategically and unconditionally loving and serving people. It is the best investment of our lives.

CONSIDER

Dream about people you know in each category listed in the chart below. Then consider a plan to intentionally pursue them.

PEOPLE YOU NEED	PLAN FOR TIME TOGETHER
Mentors	
Friends	
Family	
Other	

PEOPLE WHO NEED YOU	PLAN FOR TIME TOGETHER
Neighbors	
Coworkers	
Friends	
Family	
Outside of acquaintances (imprisoned, elderly, poor)	
Other	

How can you begin to invest more in these people? What are practical ways you can keep all your time from going to casual friendships?

DEAL

Which of the following is keeping you from meaningful friendships: (1) time, (2) fear, (3) insecurity, (4) expectations, (5) distraction, (6) lack of trust, (7) other? Write about it.

Which of the following is keeping you from engaging in relationships with those who need God: (1) time, (2) fear, (3) insecurity, (4) expectations, (5) distraction, (6) lack of trust, (7) other? How?

THREADS OF PASSIONS

*I will remove from you your heart of stone
and give you a heart of flesh.*

—EZEKIEL 36:26

William Wilberforce knew his passion. He resisted it, but this passion held him captive as a young man, nearly at the same time that he became completely captivated by Jesus. He met God and wanted nothing more than to begin vocational ministry; he was convinced this was the best way to serve God. But the passion that kept him up at night, that had him pacing floors and banging tables, was the unacceptable injustice of the slave trade in England.

His minister, John Newton, a former slave trader, enlightened him about the horrors of slavery. William was haunted. God had given him a gift for communication, the empathy of one who had suffered, a position of influence through the House of Commons, and a deep, lifelong friendship with the prime minister of England. And he was faced with a need too awful to ignore. A dozen or more threads, ordained by the hand of God, were slowly assembling into a great calling.

Finally Wilberforce's friends convinced him that God could potentially use him most in the place of politician. He ran headfirst toward the thing that haunted him. It was painful, and most of his life was spent before there was any reform.[1] But at some point his passions turned into a calling. When that happens, the cost becomes irrelevant.

Do you see the need around you?

We often miss this as a main point of the story of Joseph, but it is key. What was God doing through Joseph's decades of suffering? Was He refining Joseph? Yes. Was He restoring Joseph to his family? Yes. But ultimately God intended Joseph's life "to save many lives." And by the end of Joseph's life, he told his brothers it was all worth it.

NEED

Every Christian knows that Christ gives us a foundational calling: to live as Christ. Christ met needs. And all our other passions serve only to lead us to the unique needs we can meet. Wilberforce and Joseph weren't especially spectacular human beings; they just gave their lives to the problems of their generations. We could do that too. And together, as one body with many parts, we could see God move.

The word *passion* originates in Latin, meaning "to suffer." The word was created by religious scholars in the eleventh century to describe the willing suffering of Christ. Haven't we flipped that definition on its head? Passions have become nearly synonymous with pleasures and what excites us in modern culture. But consider that *passion* is originally defined as the moment of the deepest willing suffering of Christ for our good. This lifts the word from human desires to a monumental love willing to suffer.

When we find ourselves willing to choose suffering for a cause, that cause may hold our life's mission.

God often leads us to passions through suffering, experienced or perceived. As you considered your scars on this journey, hopefully passions began to arise out of your darkest moments. You long to give the world what you failed to receive. Passions are also born out of observing the suffering of others.

William Wilberforce observed suffering, and as it haunted him, his passions followed with a great intensity that eventually led him to his calling. Joseph suffered great pain in his life, but his suffering gave him a sincere passion for reconciliation and human care. We don't naturally have passion for others; naturally we are dang selfish. But when we were bought by Christ, we exchanged our hearts full of self-seeking passions for God's heart. And now we share His passions.

God said through His prophet,

> I will cleanse you from all your impurities and from all your idols. I will give you a new heart and put a new spirit in you; I will remove from you your heart of stone and give you a heart of flesh. And I will put my Spirit in you and move you to follow my decrees and be careful to keep my laws. (Ezek. 36:25–27)

Our hearts are new, and now what was cold is warm and full of compassion, led and moved by His Spirit. We were built for this. What begins as a burden and obligation becomes the thing that fills our restless souls.

In the movie *Amazing Grace*, William Pitt's character races through a field with Wilberforce and says to him, "Why is it you only feel the thorns in your feet when you stop running?"[2] When we run for God and for people, we forget for just a moment about ourselves, and it feels amazing. Nothing makes a soul sicker than too much time given to itself.

It's like a five-year-old who you have to force to clean up the back-yard. Every second of it seems to cause him physical anguish, until he finishes and looks up at you and says, "I am a good cleaner. That was fun." We aren't ever happy when we're lazy and selfish. The things we often think may steal our joy turn out to be the truest wells of joy that exist.

BEAUTIFUL

Just because God loves us and wanted to make life more fun for us, He built us to love different things so we could meet different needs. So my daughter Kate loves art, and Caroline would rather sing. My son Conner is smarter than most humans on earth, and Coop may be the next Emmitt Smith. And every one of them is permitted to pursue these passions for the glory of God and the love of people.

It's beautiful that your heart doesn't beat fast about the same things that make my heart beat fast. It's beautiful that your gifts are not the same as your mom's and your place is not the same as your best friend's. When we start to lay out our threads, it is unbelievable—breathtaking, really—to see how what felt average weeks ago starts to take on intricate beauty. Our untangling threads reveal God's sovereignty and attention to detail. Beautiful is the body of Christ stretched and poured out into every crevice of this world: every city, every neighborhood, every office, every home. It's the unselfish passions of people displaying the love of their God in a million unique ways.

Beautiful are all your unique threads that cause you to beat the table, or lie in bed awake, or speak with exclamation marks. Now let's see what they are.

PASSIONS

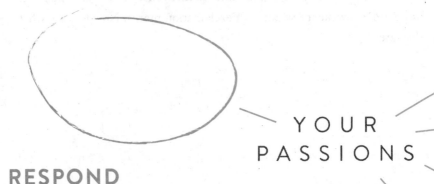

YOUR PASSIONS

RESPOND

What need do you see around you? When have you seen need that made your heart race?

When you are mad about injustice, what is happening?

When do you remember meeting a need and feeling very fulfilled?

What do you think your main passions in life are currently?

What pursuits would change in your life if you knew you did not have long to live?

FEEDING YOUR PASSIONS

*Pharaoh said to Joseph, "I had a dream, and no one
can interpret it. But I have heard it said of you that
when you hear a dream you can interpret it."
"I cannot do it," Joseph replied to Pharaoh, "but God
will give Pharaoh the answer he desires."*

—GENESIS 41:15–16

A s my real-life people in Austin and I worked through the concept of passions in one of my small groups, I glanced down and saw pages of scribbled notes in Amanda's hand. She asked her group about the need they saw around them. But it was obvious that Amanda was about to explode, so I turned the question back on her. She told us about her breakthrough.

Amanda is a speech therapist, and she has always known that her work was important to children with fairly severe disabilities, many who were unable to speak.

Deep in me, I've known I can communicate, because of my train-ing and gifts, with these kids, sometimes better than even their parents. But this week I heard from a grown man who has the same disability as many of my kids, cerebral palsy. Roger shared how alone he felt in his head because he can't really talk clearly, and how Jesus is the only reason he has not taken his life.

It was right in front of me, but for the first time I thought, *I can tell these kids about Jesus.* So I called my friend Rachel, and together we are going to host a special needs vacation Bible school this summer. Most of these families have never been to church. These kids perhaps have never heard of Jesus.

It was so simple and so beautiful. Her heart was taken captive, haunted by the need in her place, with her people, using her gifts and story of her lifetime without God. And now the Holy Spirit was leading her to her part in His story. Ordinary threads were weaving epic stories. It isn't all as complicated as we often make it.

Joseph's gift of dream interpretation finally met a need: Pharaoh needed a dream interpreted. When he brought Joseph up out of prison to explain the dream, Joseph let God work through him, saying "I cannot do it . . . but God will." Then God started weaving the threads that put Pharaoh and Joseph in a partnership. From the dream they learned they would save food throughout the famine, and their partnership would save a generation of people on the earth—meet needs, fill hungry bellies, provide work, and bring glory to God. When a gift met a need, passion was born—passion that saved many lives.

PASSION KILLERS

Nothing kills passion more than the fear of man, whether a quest for approval or nagging comparison. If we are running our race and our eyes are darting back and forth, we will not see the need around us. Hebrews

12:2 is stern about this. You want to run this race? You fix your eyes on Jesus.

As a young believer, aware of my gifts and increasingly aware of the need, I remember passion burning in my chest to teach God to the women around me but thinking, *Why would I ever teach when there are VHS tapes of Beth Moore?* I compared myself to her rather than fixing my eyes on Jesus. I was distracted from running my race in my place.

Hear me: *You have a race that no one else can run. So please run.*

"For whatever does not proceed from faith is sin" (Rom. 14:23 ESV). This is a verse that makes every one of us shudder and consider ourselves the worst of sinners. How does everything come from a place of faith? We all doubt and get fearful and wander toward lives completely absorbed with ourselves. We are unable to move without God. He moves us; we just have to let Him.

If you are anxious because you don't know your passions or don't know if you are living them, or ever could, or if you are beating yourself up because you have lived distracted, stop. We will never move forward if we . . .

- cannot love,
- cannot know God,
- cannot know ourselves,
- cannot change,
- and cannot bleed for others.

We can't move without God's Spirit moving in and through us to accomplish His purposes. We are not left as orphans to figure all this out. He is with us. That is why Jesus could say, "My yoke is easy, and my burden is light" (Matt. 11:30). He didn't call us to something alone. He carries the yoke for us, so we can run with power.

FIGHT

Nothing kills passion more than the fear of man, whether a quest for approval or nagging comparison. The biggest enemy to passion is entangling yourself in pleasing people.

How have you seen your passion affected by people (externally) or self-comparison (internally)? List a few of your main passions, and then write out how they can be affected in the columns below.

YOUR PASSIONS	APPROVAL OF MAN	COMPARISON

What are the biggest obstacles keeping you from engaging others' needs? What makes you "turn the channel"?

ACT

Often we protect our lives from observing the need around us. On your own, or with a small group of friends, family, church members, or other helpers in your life, dream of a need in your community, and together organize a time for you to serve that need.

Some examples are visiting a retirement home, serving in a soup kitchen, organizing a dinner to get to know neighbors, and sponsoring a child together. Outline these dreams in the space below.

Now pray together that these interactions will spark something for God's glory.

READ & REFLECT

Reread Genesis 41:41–56.

Describe Joseph's mission at this point.

Describe the faith that Joseph had to have in God to prepare Egypt in this way.

Read Genesis 47:13–31.

Describe the way Joseph led through the famine. What was his motivation? What were some of his passions in these verses?

How were the people around Joseph influenced by his leadership?

What stood out to you in your study of Joseph's life today?

MYSTERY

The wind blows wherever it pleases. You hear its sound,
but you cannot tell where it comes from or where it is
going. So it is with everyone born of the Spirit.

—JOHN 3:8

Shelby was confident, or so I thought. She was entering her senior year at the University of Texas, and her long blond hair and beautiful smile tricked me, concealing the truth that she was flat struggling. She was doing her best to smash together a loving God with a broken life. With freshly divorced parents and the heartbreak of a recent breakup, she wanted answers. She sat at my kitchen counter, waiting for me to ask her the question that she knew I sincerely wanted the answer to: "How are you?"

Clinging to her coffee cup as I completed the dishes, she bravely began to lay out doubts about God and her future. Then she reached for a notebook marked with questions and wrestlings, likely created in the middle of nights with no sleep.

As she glanced at her notes, she fired off questions, most of which I didn't have perfectly wrapped answers for. Then she asked one so close to home, it shook me a little.

"How do I know if I am hearing God?"

It shook me because I had so often wondered the same thing, and I had felt moved to have company in my search for this answer. God was beginning to lead me toward dreams, but I was terrified they weren't from Him. What if I stepped out and it was really just me all along?

The real question we were asking is, "Since God rarely writes in the sky, how do I know what is spiritual and supernatural, and what are just my own futile thoughts?" Trying to separate humanity from deity is no small task. It demands knowing God and then digging into what is really happening, inside of us and digging into Scripture.

From the beginning of this journey, I hope I have been clear that there is no perfect equation leading to clear and fulfilling purpose. And that is in part the brilliance of our God. Ultimately, He is the Tailor who stiches all our threads together into His larger story, and we depend on Him to do it.

DEPENDENT PRAYER

Our Savior, fully God, depending on His Father for every breath—never acting apart from His Father's will, never acting in His flesh, never bowing down to earthly desires—prayed dependently. He wanted so much to live out His Father's will that He subjected Himself to forty days without food or water or people. It was so humble and beautiful—God in the flesh . . . dependent.

Jesus knew there was a war, and the war was for us. We were to be won back, and He would choose suffering again and again until He got us back. And He prayed for us.

I am reminded of the war for my soul—the quiet, subtle, and alluring current pulling me toward doubtful independence. Prayer is hard. It is talking to someone invisible. And it helps to embrace the belief that this invisible God hears me and responds. I am not prone to talking to invisible beings.

If we are all honest, the sin of prayerlessness is common. We have a hard time sitting still with ourselves. We feel restless and cranky, and dealing with God seems daunting. But if we were asked, "Do you pray?" we would all pipe up, "Of course!" Like if someone asked us "Do you love God?" Of course.

But do we really take chunks of our days and form words in our minds, hearts, and mouths to an invisible God? Or would that "of course" be referring to mealtime or tucking in our kids? Or the tossed up "Thank you, God" as the plane lands on time and intact? Or would that "of course" be a lie because honestly you can't remember the last time you talked to God? Not about Him—to Him.

"Never stop praying" (1 Thess. 5:17 NLT). Paul suggests in this verse that our entire lives could and should be lived in belief and dependence on that invisible God. Our generation has so run from the bounds of legalism (which I applaud), that many of us have left behind all the practices designed to help us know and love our God. I want to *need* prayer and run to it with discipline and desire.

There are two sides to our war, and while one may be about to win, God is clear that we will personally and daily win only if we cling to Him. God's goal for our lives is that we would live in complete and utter surrender and dependence on Him. It is always His mercy to show us that need, whatever the cost.

REGENERATING SPIRIT

So as each of us processes how we should spend our lives, remember that nothing we have done together matters without the Spirit of God. He illumines our understanding of God and of ourselves, and He leads us daily in our prayers and in our actions. He empowers every move we will make for His glory. He is God in us, with us, for us, and through us. I do not want to spend one fleeting day here without embracing as much of God as I can.

Jesus said about the Holy Spirit,

Flesh gives birth to flesh, but the Spirit gives birth to spirit. You should not be surprised at my saying, "You must be born again." The wind blows wherever it pleases. You hear its sound, but you cannot tell where it comes from or where it is going. So it is with everyone born of the Spirit. (John 3:6–8)

When Jesus saves, we have full access to His Spirit. We have a regenerate soul.

regenerate (adj.)
formed or created again
spiritually reborn or converted
restored to a better, higher, or more worthy state[1]

It is an odd word, but it is one of my favorites because of the fact that the insides of me are completely reborn, new, different. That is the evidence of my salvation; it is the evidence of God in me, and it is the only foundation we can dream of pleasing God from. It takes away the striving and comparing I tend to turn to.

Without a new soul, without the Spirit filling us, we are just jacked-up humans.

But with His Spirit . . .

If we had only an inkling of all we miss because we do not pray, because we do not believe the Spirit in us is able to do impossible things, we would shudder. You have God in you and waiting to go crazy through you if you would just let Him.

BELIEVE

Do not leave this process without this one thing perfectly clear in your mind: Have you put your faith in the person and work of Jesus Christ for the forgiveness of sin?

If so, you are full of the Spirit of God, whether you feel Him or not. He is promised to you, and your soul is reborn, different, new, free from the bondage of sin, and free to spend your life on the purposes of God that will never fade.

If not, what is holding you back?

If so, how can you live more in the truth of what God's Spirit does for you?

Get with someone from your small group or a friend who knows God and process this. What you believe about God is the most important thing about you.

RESPOND

Are you certain that you are filled with the Spirit? Why or why not? What evidence do you see in your life that your soul is changed?

What evidence have you seen in others of a "regenerate spirit"?

Reflect on a time you felt the Spirit working in you or leading you. How did you know? In what ways do you limit the Spirit's work in your life?

Does anything keep you from praying? How can you remove that obstacle going forward?

READ & REFLECT

Read Luke 24:44–49.

This was a big moment. Jesus was telling His men exactly what had just happened, and He connected it to the prophecies. He also gave them instruction on how to proceed. In this one little paragraph, there was so much for these men to take in.

Write down each fact and command that Jesus revealed in these verses.

Why do you think He warned them about moving forward without His Spirit?

Read Acts 2.

Describe the Spirit's power in verses 17–21 and what the Spirit brings to us.

Describe Jesus from these verses.

Describe the call of God through Peter in verses 38 and 39.

Describe the lives of the people who had received the Spirit in verses 42–47.

THE TAILOR

In all your ways submit to him, and he will make your paths straight.

—PROVERBS 3:6

We do not have power to change our own souls or to change others. At times that concept has crippled and frustrated me, until its truth shifted me to freedom. I do not want to be responsible for what can only be handled and achieved by God Himself. I'm not the Tailor; I just have these threads.

It is possible that you have dug into Scripture with all your heart, and prayed for God to show His will, and laid out your threads, and done every project in this book, and you still feel unsure about your purpose. Take comfort. This is a journey that God put into motion, and He knows that He needs to tether us to Himself with the unknowns. We get all independent with what we think we know.

I remember a day when my then-thirteen-year-old son Conner walked into my room, sat down on the sofa, and said, "Mom, I need to tell you about my day." I immediately assumed he was obligated by the school principal to tell me the trouble he had incurred, but instead he started rambling about his friendships and the girl's heart he recently broke, and he wondered out loud with me how to navigate it all.

My son, for the first time in months, needed me, and he couldn't have done any more spectacular act to show his love for me.

Close your eyes, like Jesus did, and pray. Right now. Wherever you are, tell God you need Him. We forget we need Him, but He dearly loves to hear from us. And the beautiful thing is that we tend to remember when we are pouring our lives into His purposes. When we are building for Him, His Spirit reminds us we need Him every day.

I remember I need God when . . .

- I feel tangled up with sin and fear.

   For the Spirit God gave us does not make us timid, but gives us power, love and self-discipline. (2 Tim. 1:7)
- I don't know what to do.

   My sheep listen to my voice; I know them, and they follow me. (John 10:27)
- I forget.

   But the Advocate, the Holy Spirit, whom the Father will send in my name, will teach you all things and will remind you of everything I have said to you. (John 14:26)
- I am discouraged.

   In the same way, the Spirit helps us in our weakness. We do not know what we ought to pray for, but the Spirit himself intercedes for us through wordless groans. (Rom. 8:26)

We need God when we are restless, bored, numb, cold, selfish, or distracted. It won't be some great vision that will fill our souls; it will be the Spirit of the living God and Him alone.

RUNNING DEPENDENT

Let me tell you about the thirteen-year-old who melted me with the meanderings of seventh-grade life that day. Our oldest son, Conner, has always been a naturally gifted athlete. (He can thank God for accessing more of my husband's gene pool than mine while building my son.)

As good an athlete as Conner was, early in the season of every sport, he thought too hard. He played fearfully and watched the clock and the referee, and you could see him thinking about the plays and minding the rules. But then, finally, at some point in every season, he completely let go and played his guts out. Then by the last game or two, my son was playing lights-out.

It was usually sloppy, his mop of blond hair and body flopping around, but he played with such abandon in those last games that it worked. It wasn't perfect or pretty, but it was passionate and, in a way, effortless. The crowd always went wild, and Conner barely noticed because he was having so much fun.

God is after this kind of living from us, and no doubt we are craving it too. But this free, abandoned, passionate kind of life is not possible without one thing. And that one thing is perhaps the most neglected thing in all of modern Christendom. The Spirit.

THE PATTERN OF THE SPIRIT

Because people mess up in huge, destructive ways, because we are afraid we won't live well without structure, and because it feels like something is missing, we fill gaps with things we think may work: Systems. Rules. Expectations. Prescriptions.

And yet God spent the Old Testament foreshadowing something to come and the New Testament explaining what had come.

> I will put my law in their minds
>> and write it on their hearts.
> I will be their God,
>> and they will be my people. (Jer. 31:33)

Empowered. Convicted. Encouraged. Peaceful. This is the normative pattern of the Spirit of God in a person. Most of us are looking everywhere for a life like this. We are restless because we are exhausted from living in our own strength. We have come to the end of our own striving.

I do not know what you will do when you end this journey, but I trust fully in the promise of Scripture that if you commit all your ways to the Lord, He will set your path straight (Prov. 3:6). For me, that has typically looked like knowing only the exact next step in my race and trusting Him with the darkness looming ahead.

So together, let's step forward. Pursue the Tailor, and trust Him to create something good with your threads.

THE TAILOR

Spend a few hours alone somewhere quiet where
you can reconnect with God.

Talk to God about
your relationship with Him,
your need for Him,
the threads that are becoming clear,
and the unknowns of your future and purpose.

RESPOND

In what ways is it difficult for you to trust God?

What circumstances remind you that you need God?

What might God be calling you to do, and what scares you about it?

DAY 32

YOUR THREADS

*For now we see only a reflection as in a mirror; then
we shall see face to face. Now I know in part; then
I shall know fully, even as I am fully known.*

—1 CORINTHIANS 13:12

Friends, you have done a lot of soul searching. You have written about and processed God, His story, and your own story. You've explored your gifts, your scars, and your passions, and hopefully you have paused to pray and had reflective conversations over long meals with friends or family.

Now we are about to pull a lot of this together into one place. And I pray that as you lay out all the pieces of your life, patterns and passions will surface, connections will be made, and God will be more fully glorified through your threads. He is waiting to weave something beautiful out of them.

Unique design indicates unique purpose. Not one part of you exists by accident. God wants to move all of these pieces into epic stories that last forever. After you have laid out all your threads in the chart below, sit across from a few friends and/or family and hear what they say. Note the connections, have fun dreaming with them, and allow them to dream with you.

Assemble all of the threads of your life here.

THREADS

---

1. Looking back at your response pages, narrow down your
lists to the most descriptive words or phrases.

2. Put each list in its place on the following pages.

3. Brainstorm connections and patterns.
Mark up these pages. Ask God for discernment as you dream.

4. Lay your threads in front of people who know
you well and can help you dream.

THREADS

GIFTS

_____

_____

_____

_____

_____

ME

GOD'S
STORY

PEOPLE

_____ _____

_____ _____

_____ _____

_____ _____

_____ _____

(YOU NEED)   (NEED YOU)

212

SUFFERING

_____

_____

_____

_____

PASSIONS

_____

_____

_____

_____

HOLY
SPIRIT

PLACES

_____

_____

_____

_____

PURPOSE

213

DREAM

If you want to take this a step further and get some outside
perspective, gather a few friends for dinner and lay out the
pages with your threads. First, pray for discernment, and then
ask each person these questions:

What connections do you see as you look at my threads?

What ideas do you have for me as I dream about ways
God could use all of this?

What do you think is unique about what God has given me?

What are my next steps?

Where do you sense me holding back?

PART 4

THE FUTURE

UNTANGLING A DREAM

*My grace is sufficient for you, for my power
is made perfect in weakness.*

—2 CORINTHIANS 12:9

You may be thinking, as you stare and sigh and moan at your threads, that you still do not know what you are supposed to do with your life. If that is true, and everyone you love has stared at your threads with no answers, let me tell you how to find out:

Go *do something*. Anything.

Start somewhere, and through working, building, creating, and leading, you're going to learn things about yourself. I can promise you that if someone is pretty confident about the way they're wired and knows what they want to be doing, it is because they've spent significant time processing and practicing. They have also likely spent a lot of time failing at the wrong endeavors. Part of knowing where you need to be is knowing where you never need to be.

This is a process of discovering. But lean into the process. Because how we spend our lives matters.

THE UNKNOWN COST

I have friends who felt God's call to the mission field, and their house sold in two days. And I have friends who felt God's call to the mission field, and their house took two years to sell. They lost money, and everything about their lives fell apart in the meantime. Which ones really heard a call from God?

Following God, reading Him, is all so beautifully and painfully mysterious. Some of you will clearly see purpose and visions in your threads, and you will run with near certainty that they are callings from God. And some of you will barely detect a hint of a plan and will nervously step out toward a dream; it will feel almost completely dark, but you will do it.

Can God be in both?

I know there may not be complete clarity, but if your heart is willing and you want God's glory, and you give Him these pieces of your life, something will happen. He waits for us.

We all doubt and overanalyze, and to some degree, God moves anyway. He moves on with His plans on this earth with or without us. He moves our hearts toward His plans as well. What if we hadn't adopted Cooper? What if we sensed God's call and leading but didn't act? I don't know, but I do know that somehow, despite a lot of resistance from us, God did not let us miss His plans for our lives. Forever I am thankful.

Maybe these small threads are His way of making sure that you don't miss His plans for your life either. His will eventually will be done on earth as it is in heaven.

PERFECT IN WEAKNESS

When connecting all your threads, you might conclude that they are nothing special, that you've made too many mistakes, have too many weaknesses, or have lain dormant for too long. But before you allow cynicism or defeat to sneak in, listen to God's backward ways. This is the apostle Paul when he spoke of his weakness:

> But [God] said to me, "My grace is sufficient for you, for my power is made perfect in weakness." Therefore I will boast all the more gladly about my weaknesses, so that Christ's power may rest on me. That is why, for Christ's sake, I delight in weaknesses, in insults, in hardships, in persecutions, in difficulties. For when I am weak, then I am strong. (2 Cor. 12:9–10)

We will not go charge a mountain with our glorious gifts and noble passions. We will do it in our weakness so that God will get the glory.

If you feel lousy when you fill your little chart out because it feels average . . . if you find sin staring back at you next to some great calling . . . if you see the hint of a preposterous dream but think you could never ever fulfill it . . .

Brilliant. Beautiful. That is okay. That is probably exactly right.

The very things I have wished away my entire life seem to be the exact things that keep me close to God.

Do not shrink back. Build your team, dream, and allow them to speak into your life as you speak into theirs. We need kindred warriors to help us divide truth from lies, to speak courage into fear and vision into the fog.

We all are restless, all at the same time. And while we build up one another, God continues to move us to act in our places. Not because we're different or special (none of us are) but because His purposes are mind-blowingly greater than what we can imagine.

We will do the things God has built for us to do, but it won't be because we are special, great, or powerful. You will do great things because God is moving on this earth to accomplish His purposes for His glory. And honestly, in my weakness He looks good. In my usual, normal, averageness He gets credit.

I'm becoming okay with that—looking a little crazy and ridiculous while He looks awesome.

Please live your purposes. Please lay out your threads and embrace that you exist for specific purposes, and no one else can live them like you.

RESPOND

Part of knowing where you need to be is knowing where you never need to be. When have you had an experience that taught you where you never need to be? How was that valuable?

Looking at your threads, on a scale from crystal clear to completely dark, how clear are you right now on what they mean? How do you feel about it?

What might stepping out and doing "something, anything" look like, considering how clear your threads are to you?

In light of what your calling may be, list five ways you feel average or subpar.

How could God get the glory if you stepped out despite those things?

Where are you on building your team of kindred warriors? How could you make your team stronger?

READ & REFLECT

Read 2 Corinthians 12:1–10, keeping in mind your answers to today's questions.

What kept Paul from becoming conceited?

How is it possible to delight in hardships?

Was Paul okay with looking "crazy and ridiculous"? How?

After reading these passages, consider the answers to these two questions:

Who are You, Lord?

What do You want for me?

SHRINKING BACK

My righteous one will live by faith.
And I take no pleasure
in the one who shrinks back.

—HEBREWS 10:38

Zac and I sat at dinner with friends, asking them terribly intrusive questions. We want to know people's souls but have an awkward way with small talk, so we skip it. Zac asked, "What gets you excited right now?"

Immediately, Rebecca's eyes sparked, and without giving it thought, she let her words bleed about a need she saw in the American church. She had a big vision of how the need could be met. Then suddenly her eyes dropped, almost regretting what she had just revealed. She was unsure of herself and yet busting out of her skin to do something about the need she saw. She quickly pushed her passion safely and neatly back inside herself.

This was becoming a theme around me. Since signing on to write my first book, I had become a type of priest for friends' confessions of unfulfilled passions, as if watching me be brave convicted them. Nope—I should clarify. They weren't seeing me be brave; they were actually seeing me be afraid but obey anyway. And witnessing the mess of that process woke them up a little, made them uncomfortable, and made them wonder what it was they were supposed to be doing and why it was they weren't doing it.

As we were getting ready for bed after that dinner, Zac casually said, "Men are often confused about what they are supposed to do. It seems more women know deep down—they are just afraid to do it."

Something is stopping us from running wild toward our purposes. In fact, we stop ourselves. When we let our hearts run wild for a minute, we can experience a sudden shift—our eyes drop and we remind ourselves in some way that we shouldn't go there.

Why do we do this?

Because there is a war. And I wish I were being dramatic. But it's real, and you know it because you feel it too. It's a resistance that comes any time you consider doing something potentially important, and suddenly all you want to do is grab a bowl of peanut M&M's and get lost in your third viewing of *Downton Abbey*. In *The War of Art*, Steven Pressfield observed, "The more important a call or action is to our soul's evolution, the more resistance we will feel toward pursuing it."[1]

Why does it feel so hard to *not* be numb? Because there is a war waging for our hearts, to shut them down. To disable those who love Jesus, and especially those who are surrendered.

So I propose *we fight*.

The writer of Hebrews was addressing Hebrew believers who had tasted fear. They were exhausted, their friends and family had been imprisoned or killed, and they were wondering if living for Jesus was worth it. They were scared for their lives and families. They were weary.

"In just a little while, he who is coming will come and will not delay. . . . But my righteous one will live by faith. And I take no pleasure in the one who *shrinks back*" (Heb. 10:37–38, emphasis added). Let those words haunt you. I shrink back a lot, and it haunts me too. We all are plagued with inner wars:

- I shrink back because I'm afraid.
- I don't trust myself.
- I'm confused because I'm not exactly sure what it is He wants me to do.
- I don't know for sure that I can do what God wants me to do.
- I've already got too much to do right in front of me.

I don't know what it is for you, but I bet that in some way, in some place in your soul, you are shrinking back. Even though we were saved and have God with us to live our callings, we all are shrinking back. So let's go there. *Why* are you shrinking back? *Why* are you afraid to live your calling? Where do you feel the most resistance?

Physically?

- I don't have enough margin in this season of life.
- I am already strapped financially.
- I can't neglect other responsibilities.
- It's really not a big deal.
- I'm too young/too old.
- I am not 100 percent sure this is God's will.
- It's not going to make a difference.

Emotionally?

- It feels lonely.
- I crave security.
- I can't control what is going to happen.
- I am scared I'll fail.

- I am not a leader.
- I am screwed up.
- I want a comfortable life.

Relationally?

- My spouse will not support this.
- What if God takes someone I love?
- I'll look foolish.
- If I do this, I will let people down.
- My family doesn't understand.
- People think I'm crazy.
- My life will look different than my friends'.

Spiritually?

- I am not good enough for God to use me.
- I can't even pray right now.
- I don't know if I trust God's plan for me.
- Do I really believe God is real?
- I am stuck in sin.
- I don't think God even sees me.
- Is it worth it?
- What if God doesn't show up?
- What if I am misreading God?

So do the work. Ask yourself, *Why am I shrinking back?*

We get to be part of God's amazing story. It is the highest honor of our lives. Yet it is easy to read books and have moments where that feels true, and then wake up to a sink full of dishes and a job you hate, and forget. There is a war, you know, so before you set down your dream, identify why you might be shrinking back. Once you know, we'll explore how to fight.

RESPOND

Describe a way you've felt "resistance."

How might resistance help you know what's important? How else can it help you?

Name a time when you have stopped yourself. Why did you do it?

Where do you feel resistance physically? Emotionally? Spiritually? Relationally?

Do you really believe that there is a war going on? How would you describe the Enemy's status and your status in this war?

Pray for discernment. Ask God to bring up your areas of resistance and the areas in which you stop yourself so you can deal with them together in the coming days.

READ & REFLECT

Read Hebrews 10:32–12:3, keeping in mind your answers to today's questions. In your own words summarize the story of God's work on earth as told in Hebrews 10:36–12:3.

What most defined these men and women?

Define faith (Heb. 11:1).

Describe the actions of someone without faith (Heb. 10:38–39).

How did the people in today's verses live out their faith? Describe some of the things that happened because of someone's faith (Heb. 11).

What do you think was the main thing God was accomplishing on earth through these generations of people? They didn't have the Helper Jesus promised (John 14:15–18). Even Joseph didn't. What does that tell us about God's love and provision then and now?

What is the "something better" He planned (Heb. 11:40)? Why can we have confidence and pray for discernment expectantly?

After reading these passages, consider the answers to these two questions:

Who are You, Lord?
What do You want for me?

FIGHT FOR IT

Consider him who endured such opposition from sinners,
so that you will not grow weary and lose heart.

—HEBREWS 12:3

O nce you know where you're shrinking back, you can take the fight to the next level. You can fight on the front lines, shutting down the enemies of your heart and your dreams. The common enemies of fear, uncertainty, distraction, and insecurity must not be allowed to run free in your life. You can fight them.

FIGHT FEAR

I shrink back because I'm afraid. I am afraid of what I will lose. What if following God costs me the things I love most? What if He takes my spouse or child? What if I lose approval or comfort or success or control? What if I give my life, and He takes away the deepest desires of my heart?

I feel the fear when pulling the trigger on a dream that only someone stupid or possessed by God would dare to dream. I am terrified. This could fail. This may not even be from God. And I am going to do it anyway.

We have to deal with fear because it could possibly make us miss the best parts of life. We all face it, but we must kill fear like it is the Devil because it usually is. We do not belong to the one who shrinks back; we belong to the One who moved through His blood and sweat and despair and fear and reluctance in the garden of Gethsemane and said, "Not my will, but Yours be done. I belong to You, and I will live for You and die for You." He walked headfirst into His death. So fight with me.

FIGHT UNCERTAINTY

I shrink back because I'm unclear. Honestly, I have never known anything with 100 percent certainty. God's will usually is revealed after something happens. Were we 100 percent sure we were supposed to adopt Cooper? No. We just had a burden we couldn't shake, and at some point when that burden lines up with Scripture, you have to ask yourself, "Is this God?"

You won't believe how much you actually *do* know. And we have a thick book from God about who He is and what He wants for us that we can absolutely trust. But honestly, there is a lot we know about ourselves. He likes His kids completely hanging on to Him for dear life more than He cares about the perfect plan being executed. He is after *us*, and uncertainty is usually what keeps us glued to His side.

He is in the trenches with us. In the fear. In the uncertainty. He is in the unknown—knowing and leading and working. What we don't know yet is meant to lead us to dependence.

FIGHT DISTRACTION

I shrink back because I'm distracted. I've already got too much to do right in front of me. We have to be the most distractible generation on earth. There is just so much out there fighting for our attention.

I have four kids, church, friends, and dry cleaning, and everybody around me seems to need to eat all the time. I have a pretty full-time job in ministry, and on and on like everyone else. But somehow I still manage to watch every season of my favorite shows, use Facebook to keep up with people I haven't seen in fifteen years, and take a lot of baths and a few naps. And there is not necessarily anything wrong with any of it—the things I have to do, and the things I want to do, and the things I just need so my soul doesn't shrivel up. But if I do all of it and never consider that there is a bigger reason I am here, I could be missing the point—missing the Only Thing for all the small things.

All things are permissible but not all things are beneficial (1 Cor. 10:23). There is an art to living that is far above the base human instinct of survival. I want to live beautifully. I want to live slowly and breathe in every moment. Let's make that kind of beautiful life. Without distraction, without wasting a minute.

FIGHT INSECURITY

I shrink back because I'm insecure. Every single time I stand up in front of ten people or ten thousand, I tremble. I shake. I have a very physical reminder of my insecurity. And I've learned to not wish it away. My insecurity makes me pray every time. When I get on my knees, God reminds me that this is about Him and not me. He reminds me that I have nothing to prove anymore.

Because of grace, we have nothing to prove. Our confidence is in the security and power God gives us, not in ourselves. To know that we are absolutely treasured, unconditionally, changes us. We feel free and want to run with a God who would love like that. To know that we do not measure up and that we don't have to because of Jesus, because of grace, means that life gets a whole lot more fun.

FIGHT COMPARISON

It is nearly impossible to do anything with our threads while we are looking side to side. Rather than listening to God alone, we look around and compare and allow our inadequacies to consume us. Then it's over before it starts.

We want a revolution, but most of us wish someone else would start it. We're embarrassingly cynical, and we shoot down leaders for sport, so no wonder we're all afraid to lead! Let's help one another fight our fears rather than taking one another down. We must focus on our races and cheer others toward theirs.

If we could cheer for one another instead of criticize, obey instead of compare, and fear God instead of men, we could watch God just flat show off in front of us.

We need one another, and we are killing one another. In Hebrews 12, the writer pleads with those who are shrinking back:

Since we are surrounded by such a great cloud of witnesses,
[We have each other.]
let us throw off everything that hinders and the sin that so easily entangles.
[Because we are free.]
And let us run with perseverance the race marked out for us,
[We have a marked race—each of us. We can't miss it for fear.]
fixing our eyes on Jesus, the pioneer and perfecter of faith. For the joy set before him he endured the cross, scorning its shame, and sat down at the right hand of the throne of God . . . so that you will not grow weary and lose heart. (vv. 1–3)

We fall apart when we look at our fears and inadequacies and compare ourselves to every other runner. But fix your eyes on a God like Jesus, and you will not quit. You will not shrink back. Not from others, and not from yourself.

Risk something. Step out and fail. Be the fool. Build a life that needs our God.

RESPOND

Flip back to yesterday and look at your resistances. How do they fall into the categories of fear, uncertainty, distraction, or insecurity?

When do you feel fear? How is "do it anyway" a way to fight it?

When do you feel uncertainty? How do your burdens line up with Scripture? Spend some time searching the Bible and reflect on what God may be saying to you.

What are your favorite distractions? Your least favorite? Are they beneficial or contributing to you missing the point?

When do you feel the most insecure?

In what practical ways would it free you to know that you don't measure up, and you don't have to because of Jesus?

READ & REFLECT

Read Hebrews 12:1–3 and review Hebrews 11, keeping in mind your answers to today's questions.

Think back to yesterday's reading about the history of faith. The author of Hebrews had a goal for the readers. He wanted them to understand the history of God on earth for a reason. What was his goal in sharing this history of faith (Heb. 12:1–3)?

If Jesus is the "perfecter of our faith," that means we can take Him an imperfect faith and let Him perfect it. How does that help us not grow weary?

If the world tells us to find joy in the race, in the journey, by setting our eyes on what's around us, how are these instructions different?

What does this imply about our race? About our response to resistance?

After reading these passages, consider the answers to these two questions:

Who are You, Lord?
What do You want for me?

WHEN WE DREAM

So then, my friends, because of God's great mercy to us I appeal to you:
Offer yourselves as a living sacrifice to God, dedicated to his service
and pleasing to him. This is the true worship that you should offer.

—ROMANS 12:1 GNT

Many women I know are keenly aware of the "rules" to being a respected woman in the worlds they inhabit. In some places, these rules might go something like this:

1. Stay home full time with the kids.
2. Don't pursue your own passions and dreams or take risks; it's selfish.
3. Volunteer as a homeroom mom.
4. Don't miss a game for any of the five sports each of your four kids plays—or a party or a field trip.
5. Dinner should be worthy of a Pinterest pinning and should be on the table by six o'clock every night.

Obviously some of the most powerful ministry on this earth is happening through stay-at-home moms and homeroom moms and at Pinterest-worthy dinners at six o'clock. These things are noble and not the problem. These tasks, and thousands of others, have to get done in homes, schools, and offices, whether we feel passionate about them or not. The problem is not in these roles or duties; the problem is when they turn into man-made rules *mandatory* for godly women.

This leaves us women feeling we can't do anything out of this acceptable box, and it strangles our souls, dreams, and obedience to God.

These expectations might be common in the South in a conservative church, but I have another friend who lives in New York City. She feels judged because she *doesn't* work outside her home and has chosen to homeschool her kids, even though those decisions are based on her personal convictions and callings. And I have another friend who has felt judged for choosing to adopt a child as a single woman. Yet another friend is drowning in toddlerhood and feels judged for not having the capacity to do anything but be sure her kids stay alive.

This is happening in a million forms in a million places. The rules seem to change in each church, each city, each country, even throughout history in each generation. Unique versions of handbooks describing "how to be a godly woman" seem to exist wherever I go.

Women, we are so dang hard on one another. We have to stop.

Our generation is laced with social and gender pressures. The weight of "the rules" for women in the church, home, and workplace is so heavy, I think we forget how all the different pressures are carried into nearly every choice we make, nearly every dream we dream.

If we are all obeying God with our unique gifts and visions, our dreaming, our obedience, then our roles should look beautifully diverse. We each look unique on the outside, and I assure you that we are even more intricately designed on the inside.

TENSIONS

What are some of the tensions you feel as a woman?

Here are some examples:

- My husband feels threatened when I dream.
- I feel like I am wasting an expensive education, but I am called to stay at home to raise my kids.
- My gifts are so strong that I am worried if I really succeed as a strong woman, no man will want to marry me.
- My kids are going to be wounded if I can't be present at everything for them.
- People don't like strong women.
- I want to go overseas, but I need to wait until I get married.
- I have to provide for my kids as a single mom; there is no one else. Dreaming is not a luxury I can afford.
- I have gifts of teaching or leadership that my church doesn't encourage women to use.
- My elderly parents need me, and/or my grandkids need me. This isn't my dream, but this is my reality, and it is all I have time for.
- I feel called to adopt and my husband doesn't.
- I can't do it all.

So what do we do?

As God called me into a more public and demanding ministry, I saw the writing on the wall: Some games were going to be missed. Sitters would become part of my family. My husband might be overshadowed by my calling at times. I would have to travel. My strong gifts would hit many ceilings within the church. I was turning in the title I had proudly worn for more than a decade: stay-at-home mom.

So many tensions lay on top of my calling because of my gender. I spent a bit of time wishing away my gender, but since that wasn't happening, I found myself wishing away my calling.

Our views of our roles are shaped by our culture and by approving or disapproving messages. What do we do when faced with these tensions?

OBEY GOD

The clearest way to obey God is through studying and applying His Word. But "obey Scripture." I wish it were simple. Nearly every respected teacher and theologian defines the roles of women from Scripture differently.

I will do my best to obey God within the boundaries and freedom Scripture gives me as a woman. But the roles of women are sometimes hard to determine in Scripture, so we should build our convictions and then give grace in the gray spaces. Personal convictions cannot become law.

We must separate biblical mandates from cultural Christian values.

TRUST GOD WITH THE COST

I felt physically burdened from worry that my kids would suffer because of God's calling on my life. And if I am honest, they have. This calling wasn't just on my life; it would go on to cost something from my entire family. Every calling has a cost.

As women, we often foresee the cost to ourselves and the people we love, and we stop. But there's something beautiful in showing the people you love how to live squarely in your purpose for God's glory. They have a chance to see God moving through you.

You may think your calling isn't as spiritual. Your cost may be a financial sacrifice because you are leaving your job, or maybe you will find yourself laying in a hotel room telling your kids about a sales conference over the phone. But whatever the calling and whoever it is costing, we are all living out the purposes of God for His glory here, in unique places with unique demands. And God calculates the costs of our callings. We don't need to be afraid of the price we'll pay; we just need to weigh it and not forfeit our God-given responsibilities for selfish gain.

I've realized my kids didn't need me at every game. They need parents who fear and obey God first. But if they saw me neglecting them out of vain ambition . . . kids are smart; I imagine they would be wounded right now. We are a family on mission together: supporting one another, sacrificing for one another, and building the name of God here in our own ways.

I want my kids to be brave and willing to obey, even if that means sacrifice. I have to model that first. Trusting God with the cost, keeping our motives His, we can be brave. You can be brave.

RESPOND

What would you say are your top five "rules" for a woman in your world? Which ones did others make for you? Which ones did you make yourself?

Do you ever feel you are not living up to them?

How do you perceive women being hard on one another? How are they hard on you? How are you hard on them?

Have you ever wished away your gender? Or have you wished away your calling instead? Why?

How might the fact that you are in your place as a woman bring even more glory to God?

How do you differentiate between personal convictions and Scripture when it comes to obeying God as a woman?

Have you ever felt the cost was too high to those you loved? What costs are you calculating when you consider your dream? What would it be like to trust God with them?

READ & REFLECT

Read Acts 5:17–41, keeping in mind your answers to today's questions.
Why did God set the apostles free in verses 19–25?
What was the cost for the apostles' preaching? To them? To others?
What rules did they break? Why did they break them?
In verses 38–39, what was the reasoning for the apostles being released?
How does this reasoning keep us close to God as we calculate our costs?

After reading these passages, consider the answers to these two questions:

Who are You, Lord?
What do You want for me?

THE VOICES WE LISTEN TO

There is neither Jew nor Gentile, neither slave nor free, nor is there male and female, for you are all one in Christ Jesus.

—GALATIANS 3:28

Our heads get so crowded. There are opinions shouting out everywhere, from parents, pastors, spouses, friends, and coworkers. If we let them all decide who we are and what we do with our lives, it gets way too crowded.

We feel so confused and wonder why we can't hear God. The thing is, we have to decide who we will listen to. So when I dream or sense some direction, I take that to my people: Scripture. The Holy Spirit. My husband. My elders and mentor. My small group of friends who love God deeply and aren't afraid to kick me in the tail or push me to obey, even if my obedience looks different from theirs. To these voices I submit; I receive truth and I count the cost.

Pick your voices and then be prepared and willing to disappoint the rest. We have to decide whom we will listen to and whom we won't. You are not obligated to bend to the convictions and judgment of every person around you, or you will never do anything. Choose to obligate yourself to a few trusted voices.

When my few voices affirm and release me, I run. And when they pull me in, I stop and listen.

A DREAM-RELEASING SPOUSE

The main earthly voice in my life is my husband. I often am asked, "As a mother and pastor's wife and writer . . . how do you do it all?" I have a lot of help: sitters and help with cleaning and administrative help. But the most obvious answer is that without the blessing, leadership, and sacrifice of my husband, with all I have in my life, I would be unable to do any of it. We have fought our way to a good marriage, and it has not been easy. But as passionate and strong and independent as I can be, it actually feels so good to come under his leadership.

There isn't a doubt that the measure of support we feel from our husbands, if we are married, will and should affect our dreams. I asked Zac to share his road to releasing and leading me to use my gifts and fulfill my callings. Here's what he had to say to husbands:

A Letter from Zac

In the midst of sixteen years of marriage, many moves, four kids, mortgages, and unfulfilling jobs, the dreams we dreamed on many dates before marriage quickly gave way to a lot of weighty responsibility.

I went from trying to win this girl's heart and longing for her freedom to pursue God's dreams for her, to actually using the Bible's language of submission to kill any dream that would inconvenience or threaten me. So, not long after the wedding day, Jennie found herself with a passive-aggressive, emotionless husband, and her God-given passions and dreams began to die.

At the time, I thought I was right and biblically justified in my "leadership" of Jennie. But I was wrong. I had memorized "Wives, submit yourselves to your own husbands" (Eph. 5:22), but had no clue of what it meant for husbands to *nourish and cherish* their wives.

Honestly, it took years for me to grow in maturity to see my error. And if you find yourself reading this and realizing you no longer have a clue how to nourish and cherish, take courage; neither do countless other men reading this letter that their wives asked them to read. Know first that my goal is not to beat you down, but rather to call you to one of the most noble callings of your life.

Husbands, don't miss this: to nourish and cherish *your wife* means taking the initiative to shepherd her gifts and callings and to help her dream.

It took me years to realize the problem wasn't being married to a passionate, gifted, "unsubmissive" wife who would start using her gifts only to have me reel her back into reality. The problem was me: my misunderstanding of my role to lead us as a team on mission, and my resentment of seeing my wife walking in freedom while I was immersed in my own insecurities.

Husbands, if you are still reading this, I believe you really want your wife to be all she is designed to be in Christ. And I believe you want to affirm her God-given dreams and callings.

So how do you become a dream-releasing husband?

- *Realize you have nothing to prove.* If you are in Christ, you have nothing left to prove. Jesus fulfilled your desperate desire to measure up. The more that truth sinks in, the less you will look to your job or money or your wife for fulfillment. Dream-releasing husbands are secure in Christ.

- *Take hold of your role.* Realize that your call to nourish and cherish your wife does not depend on her performance. As you become more secure in your own identity in Christ, you will begin to experience the joy of seeing your wife use her gifts and respond to her callings.

- *Embrace the loss of control.* As you become more secure in Christ and begin cheering on your wife to use her gifts too, you will feel a new tension surface: a life that feels semi-chaotic. You realize that what you had been calling "balance" for your family was really a determined effort to control your life at all costs. You see, God never promises balance. So this new life that feels semi-chaotic is likely a symptom of a couple attempting to follow the leading of the Holy Spirit. And no matter chaos, you will be full of joy because Jesus is infinitely more satisfying than the god of control.

Men, husbands, this is God's call on our lives. It is one of the noblest callings on the planet. And I'll bet, in the midst of your leading courageously, you will rediscover the woman you fell in love with.

—Zac

Women, as you read, know that there were many years when I did not feel released to use my gifts. And in my insecurity, I fought for my rights and nagged for my freedom. That didn't work. Our marriage became healthy again with a lot of time and prayer and counseling and surrender. We are having a lot of fun these days. It is worth the work.

Scripture talks about a day when there will no longer be slave or free,

Jew or Greek, male or female. But that day hasn't come yet. These tensions won't last forever. As a woman, I pray that my daughters' worth and identities aren't based on how they perform roles as a mother or a daughter or a wife or a friend or an employee. I pray that their souls are steadied and secure because their eyes are laser-focused on the One who built and rescued their souls. I pray this for all of us.

RESPOND

Whose voices do you find yourself listening to? Whose is the loudest?

Which people will you decide not to listen to?

React to the statement, "You are not obligated to bend to the convictions and judgment of every person around you, or you will never do anything." Have you ever felt you were bending to everyone around you? What was it like?

Who do you feel released and affirmed by?

If you are married, have you experienced tensions with your husband about your dreams? How can you address that tension?

What work will you have to do to promote dream-releasing relationships in your life?

READ & REFLECT

Read Colossians 3, keeping in mind your answers to today's questions.

Who is the ultimate authority in our lives (vv. 1–4, 17, 23)?

What are the characteristics of God's chosen people (vv. 12–17)?

How do those characteristics inform the instructions for Christian households in verses 18–25?

How do those characteristics define a relationship that has been "raised with Christ"?

What are the key components of teaching and admonishment in verse 16?

After reading these passages, consider the answers to these two questions:

Who are You, Lord?

What do You want for me?

FOCUSED AND STEADY

Fight the good fight of the faith. Take hold of the
eternal life to which you were called.

—1 TIMOTHY 6:12

I heard the call.

Gather and equip your generation.

I wasn't sure it was God, so I pushed it away for years. I had no means of doing such a preposterous thing—gathering a generation. It was ridiculous. I should clarify: I didn't grow up charismatic enough. I didn't live expecting visions from God.

I was busy living out a huge calling already: motherhood. I held no connections and no aspirations to build a platform or even write a book. Years passed, and I don't remember even thinking much about that night.

And now, after more than half a decade, I somehow find myself with so many people and threads in place, I actually consider that perhaps the whisper was from God. One night, with painful fear, God and I launched a vision to reach a generation. We called it the IF:Gathering. I expect it will take a while, and I expect to not quite get to every person on earth in our generation. But we'll try.

I wish the threads were more perfectly untangled. I'm in process and doing my best to listen to God's Spirit and respond in obedience, despite the insanity of it all. Thank God that He builds His plans on this earth in spite of us.

At nearly the same time, my football-coach-turned-pastor husband, who loves to start things and has spent the last fifteen years of his life in vocational ministry, was feeling his threads and God's Spirit rerouting him to the marketplace. He dreamed with his best friend about using business as ministry, and what it would look like to launch businesses as they invest deeply into the lives of the men they are working beside.

As I was being called deeper into vocational ministry, Zac was being called out into ministry through business. God's stories may lead to you getting paid as a pastor or as a clerk at a clothing shop, raising children or teaching them math, displaying Him through excellence as a writer of news or theology. He is creative like that, God is.

So what now?

What if you live like this?

What if you run?

What if you dream God's dreams?

What if you obey in your unique, beautiful spot?

RUN FOR YOUR LIFE

Austin's city slogan is "Keep Austin Weird." And Austin loves races. Nearly everyone who lives there has run a race. They even have races where people throw paint at you and races that drag you through obstacle courses. There is one weird race in Austin called "Run for Your Lives." It's a zombie race. People dressed up like zombies chase you and try to attack you while you run.

I haven't run in it, but I can promise you I would get a decent time in that race. I would book it if zombies were chasing me. So would you.

And in similar odd fashion, I expect if you are running your race, whatever it is, the Enemy is on your tail. Even if you are on a more defined, marked path, this race is long. This race is hard.

In the hardest, most despairing times, I felt an almost physical weight pushing me down, and I daydreamed about quitting my race—playing it over and over in my head, justifying it over and over.

I still loved God.

But I did not want to keep running. I wanted to be comfortable more than I wanted God's will for my days.

Simultaneously, our children led us to the emergency room four times in two months. One trip was life-threatening, one was brain-threatening, and one may still be a chronic illness. My grandmother was placed in hospice and was processing death with my mother, while my best friend lay upstairs on another floor of the hospital in her room, unable to move, unable to talk.

You know how life goes like that sometimes.

Was it a spiritual attack? I don't know. It did feel like zombies were on our tail. I will say if it is you, Devil, *it is below the belt to mess with my kids.*

What I do know: there is a very real and active battle, and the prize is faith. God gives faith and Satan steals faith. God loves faith more than any other thing in us, and Satan hates our faith more than any other thing.

Faith is the measure to which we believe God is God. And faith is the measure to which we let God be God.

We were living a little more bravely and obediently, and it felt like something or someone was threatened by it. By this journey, this project. It turns out, this is a marathon—not for faint souls and not for those seeking easy and happy quickly. And as I wanted to quit, my people reminded me of my God. We need our people. And the needs I saw around me whispered to me to not stop.

"WIN THE DAY"

Zac, of course, still follows football like any good Texas boy, and he passed me the story of Chip Kelly, the Oregon Ducks football coach. Coach Kelly has a saying that has almost become the slogan of the entire state. And I suggest we make it ours too: "Win the day."

Don't dream of winning Super Bowls or even Saturday's game on Monday morning. Win practice that day, in that moment. Win that day, whatever it holds.

Will our little tribe of missionaries (that we hope you will join) reach a generation? I don't know.

But today, I'll spend a few moments alone with God and really talk to Him. And I'll write you these words and send a few e-mails and hop on a few seemingly insignificant calls and spend time with my children. I'll sweep the cereal crumbs up from breakfast and cheer for my husband as he takes some financial risks to follow God. Even though I'm scared and kind of want to say, "Heck no." Even though every piece of today feels small.

I'll do today, glancing up and remembering a race is completed the same way a book is completed. Step by step. Word by word. Day by day.

Bill Gates said, "People often overestimate what will happen in the next two years and underestimate what will happen in ten."[1] Don't underestimate obedience over a long time.

Joseph swept his floors, sat on his prison floor, made strategies for farmers, built storehouses, and dreamed dreams. And somehow, he died having saved many lives and honoring God in his generation.

Great people don't do great things. God does great things with surrendered people. And surrender happens every day in one thousand small moments.

Win the day. Run the steps in front of you today.

RESPOND

What feels preposterous about the dreams you're staring down?

Might any of the callings you feel you're already living have to change?

Have you experienced any attacks from the Enemy regarding new dreams? What were they? How does faith help us fight the battle?

What would it mean for you to "win the day" today? What steps in front of you seem small or insignificant?

Dream a little. If "people often overestimate what will happen in the next two years and underestimate what will happen in ten," what could you be underestimating?

Take a look at the next five days. What small steps can you identify that will help inch you forward toward your dream?

READ & REFLECT

Read 1 Timothy 6:11–16 and 2 Peter 3:8–13, keeping in mind your answers to today's questions.

How does understanding God's perception of time affect our perception of time? How does it affect our faith?

How do we fight the good fight of faith? How long must we do this?

Until Jesus, we can only go day by day. Your thousand small moments are adding up to eternity.

After reading these passages, consider the answers to these two questions:

Who are You, Lord?

What do You want for me?

DAY 39

LEAVING BEHIND/ MOVING TOWARD

If anyone is in Christ, the new creation has come:
The old has gone, the new is here!

—2 CORINTHIANS 5:17

Sometimes it's helpful to see where we've been and where we're going, just to get perspective. I have found this to be helpful in my work with groups. Flipping back through this book and recalling your journey, take a breather and think of the things you are leaving behind and the things you are moving toward. If at any point you feel confusion or frustration in the days to come, refer back to this list, add to it, and pray over it.

So what are you leaving behind? And what are you moving toward?

Here are some examples from others who have been through this project.

LEAVING BEHIND	MOVING TOWARD
fear, anxiety	freedom in Christ
rules that shackle	freedom
Satan's foothold in my life	my King
this world	eternity
comparing myself to others	joyfully giving more of myself
restlessness	doing something *big*
insecurity	meeting others' needs around me
fear	facing the unknown with the One who does know
fear of man	watching God transform lives
fear	boldness
shame and exhaustion	"break me whole"
comfort	faith
discouragement	complete surrender
being paralyzed	fulfillment in God's purpose for me
my shallow faith	deep waters with Jesus
insecurity	wild abandon
fear and comfort	Jesus and others
judgment	having faith in what God can do, and just doing it
fear	obedience and trust
fear	whatever is ahead of time
worrying that God wasn't calling me	recruiting more leaders to run together to Christ
comfort idol	trust
apathy	intentionality
restlessness	doing something (fix your eyes on Jesus and move)
busyness	listening
anonymity	intimacy
discouragement	absolute trust
guilt	freedom
approval	Jesus and where the Holy Spirit leads
muddy dreams	needs of people right in front of me

I AM LEAVING BEHIND	I AM MOVING TOWARD

RESPOND

What are you most excited about leaving behind? About moving toward?

What are you most afraid of?

In what ways will you have to depend on God to do these things?

Reflect on how your perspective of what you can and can't do has shifted since the first week of your journey.

What verses and principles from our study of Scripture will you refer back to for strength and focus? List them here.

THE END OF MUNDANE

*We declare God's wisdom, a mystery that has been hidden
and that God destined for our glory before time began.*

—1 CORINTHIANS 2:7

We've done important work together, and no matter your *anything* prayer, your places, your people, your threads, hear me: you live in a world that is dark and craving light. People's eyes are starving for God, dying for freedom.

Your view of your life may be small, but nothing about your life is small.

Every moment is granted for purposes we can't see. Every breath is issued for eternal things left undone. We brush against people in checkout lines who will live forever in heaven or hell, and we contain God. Try to tell me your life is insignificant. Try to tell me that anything about this life is insignificant.

Feel the weight of the calling you have received, but not so you feel guilt. So that you feel great worth in your soul and in the work of your day.

THE WEIGHT OF GLORY

We are souls undone and rebuilt by the Spirit of God. As God surveys this earth, He sees light and darkness. And He sees *His* light, His Spirit wandering through neighborhoods, offices, schools, Walmarts, Chick-fil-A playgrounds, and eating breadsticks at Olive Gardens. We possess God and are filled with Him for the very same purposes that Peter, John, Paul, Mary, and Luke in the early church were filled with Him. We are filled with God to pour Him into the darkness, pour Him into the broken souls who are starving for something.

There are no average, small dreams, and no average people. There are no meaningless moments as we go to the gym or cook macaroni or handle shipping orders gone wrong or nurse our babies. If we were sitting across from one another and you pleaded with me—*begged* me—to believe you were average, your life was boring, there was nothing significant to anything you were doing, you could not convince me. You could not.

There are moments with tangled threads over dinners, where simple visions are affirmed and neighborhood boot camps are born. There are moments in speech therapy offices when you hug a mother who is fighting back tears because she wonders if her autistic toddler will get to go to mainstream kindergarten. There are many moments of sweeping up crumbs from breakfast, moments that no one sees and couldn't possibly matter except that as order is brought from chaos, your family flourishes a little more that day.

There are moments in offices, when you swallow all pride as co-workers gossip and misrepresent you to others, and God draws near in the very moment you have never felt so alone. There are moments in hospital waiting rooms when the world turns upside down, when you can shake your fist and fall down. In the darkest moments, God was building the very brightest ones.

Do you feel restless?

There is more. A story too weighty and beautiful to bear. A story stretched out beyond ten million years from today.

I feel a weight of glory.

An indescribable burden.

A holy, God-given passion burning in my soul for you, for us, for our time here. Because I know we will blink and be together with God forever, and there is life to be lived here.

C. S. Lewis said in his perfectly titled book *The Weight of Glory,* "To please God . . . to be a real ingredient in the divine happiness . . . to be loved by God, not merely pitied, but delighted in as an artist delights in his work or a father in a son—it seems impossible, a weight or burden of glory which our thoughts can hardly sustain. But so it is."[1]

So it is. We are:

- built by God
- rescued by God
- filled with God
- pleasing to God

May we never get over it. This weight of glory we carry is the promise of more, the promise of kingdoms coming that our imaginations can't contain.

So don't waste your days any longer, staring at ceilings, wondering if there is more.

There is more. Take the threads of your life and go live like it.

RESPOND

Do you believe that nothing about your life is small? Why or why not?

Describe a few of your "moments" in the past few days. Can you see how you could pour God into moments like these?

How does it affect you that you are . . .

built by God?

rescued by God?

filled with God?

pleasing to God?

In the future, if you find yourself wondering if there is more, what will you tell yourself?

How is *anything* a prayer we never stop praying?

What small things can you do to promote flourishing around you today?

How can you begin to embrace and more fully feel the "weight of glory" as it's described here?

What have you discovered during these forty days? What has surprised you?

How have you changed during these forty days?

When you wake up tomorrow, what will it look like for you to take your threads and live for more?

HOW TO FIND GOD

I can't imagine a more restless feeling than being unsure about the meaning of life and the future of my soul. As long as we are on this earth, we will ache for something bigger because we were designed for something bigger—something better. We are designed for an intimate relationship with God forever.

Saint Augustine said, "You have made us for Yourself, and our hearts are restless until they find their rest in You."[1]

We had a perfect relationship with God until sin entered the world through Adam and Eve. And with sin came the promise of death and eternal separation from God. But from the moment of the first sin, God issued a promise that would bring us back to Him.

The penalty had to be paid.

Our sin was to be placed on a perfect sacrifice. God would send His own blameless, perfect Son to bear our sin and suffer our fate—to get us back.

Jesus came fulfilling thousands of years of prophecy, lived a perfect life, and died a gruesome death, reconciling our payment for our sin. Then after three days, He defeated death, rose from the grave, and now is seated with the Father, waiting for us.

Any of us who accept the blood of Jesus for the forgiveness of our sin are adopted as a child of God and issued God's very own Spirit to seal and empower us to live this life for Him.

Our souls are restless until they rest in God. We were made for Him, and He gave everything so that our souls could finally and forever rest in Him.

If you have never trusted Christ for the forgiveness of your sins, you can do that this moment. Just tell Him about your need for Him and tell Him of your trust in Him as your Lord and Savior.

ACKNOWLEDGMENTS

First, I want to tell you a story. We needed to land on a design for the cover of this book. It was past time, and the dozens of designs I'd seen were not exactly right for this project. I was praying and wondering if I would need to go ahead and settle on a cover, when I thought about my dear friend, who, just the week before, had hung six beautiful paintings in my living room. Attached was a note that included the six prayers she had prayed over each member of my family as she painted. Her prayers were so specific and exactly what each of us needed.

Lindsey's paintings are the very first thing I see when I walk in the door, and I find myself smiling every single time I see them because they are so happy, so fun, so beautiful.

We had about one hour till we had to pull the trigger on this cover, so I picked up the phone and called my artist friend. I told her the desperate situation we were in and asked if she would be willing to let us use one of her works on the cover. She laughed and said, "Of course!"

I hung up with tears as I thanked God because she was perfect. It wasn't just the joy and beauty of this cover and her art. She was perfect because, Lindsey Meyer, you are this book.

You are one who looked around and saw raw materials and bravely created with them. You surrender daily in obedience in big ways, like adoption, and in small ways, like taking a meal to your neighbor, constantly.

You are one who takes her passion and turns it into kingdom-building prayers that shift lives.

Thank you for not only creating such a beautiful cover but for living such a beautiful life.

———

I can't believe I get to do this!

I love building tools for people to know and love God. But it wouldn't be possible without an army of people beside me, helping me build. First, to my husband, Zac, who constantly helps me dream further and care deeper and run faster than I ever would even want. You are a force for the kingdom, and you are my best friend to boot! Thanks for being a dream-releasing man. I love you forever.

To my kids, Conner, Kate, Caroline, and Coop. Thanks for cheering me on; rather than resenting what I do, you champion it and support it. Thank you for being such pictures of this book in my real life. You are what so many of my threads were weaving into and a great way to invest my life.

Chloe Hamaker, my teammate and partner in crime. I would not be able to do half of what I do without your constant support and endless work. You are evidence of God's love to me, how you serve and serve and serve and build and build and build! You could run your own ministry, but you have chosen to give these years to help build with me, and I know it's God's gift to me! Thank you, friend, for all you did to make this book helpful.

Debbie Wickwire, thank you for always believing in God in me. Thank you for jumping and getting your hands on this and making it happen! You are such a faithful editor and friend, and heaven will be fun for you because of the countless ways you have changed the world behind thousands of books.

Curtis Yates and all of the Yates and Yates team, you go so far and above in everything you do. I feel overwhelmed that God placed me in your agency. Literally, this project happened because you made it happen! Thank you for caring that these words go out further than I could ever imagine or dream.

Jennifer McNeil, you worked tirelessly to help create something helpful. Thank you for caring and working so hard. I am proud of this work, and that is because of your sacrifices as an editor to pull this off with me! Grateful for Paula Major and Natalie Nyquist for their editorial work as well and for Kristen Andrews for art directing. Thank you Daisy Hutton and W Publishing Group for continuing to believe in me and this work! I love building beside you.

NOTES

DAY 1: PRAYING *ANYTHING*
1. You can read her life-changing story at https://katiemajors.blog/.
2. Quoted in Mark Fackler, "The World Has Yet to See . . . ," *Christian History* 25 (1990), accessed August 27, 2018, https://www.christianitytoday.com /history/issues/issue-25/world-has-yet-to-see.html.

DAY 4: ANYTHING FOR HIS GLORY
1. John Piper, "Rebuilding the Basics: The Centrality of the Glory of God," desiringGod.org, November 4, 2009, https://www.desiringgod.org/articles /rebuilding-the-basics-the-centrality-of-gods-glory.

DAY 7: PERMISSION TO DREAM
1. *Merriam-Webster's Dictionary*, s.v. "dream," updated August 17, 2018, https://www.merriam-webster.com/dictionary/dream.

DAY 9: SURRENDER IS SCARY
1. Bill Bright, "Bill Bright Transcript," Crosswalk.com, March 28, 2002, https://www.crosswalk.com/faith/spiritual-life/bill-bright-transcript-1129622. html.

DAY 11: PURELY DEVOTED
1. Timothy Keller, *Every Good Endeavor: Connecting Your Work to God's Work* (New York: Penguin, 2014), 47.

DAY 13: WHAT WE CAN KNOW AND WHAT WE CAN'T
1. Kevin DeYoung, *Just Do Something* (Chicago: Moody Publishers, 2009).
2. John Piper, "How Can I Discern the Specific Calling of God on My Life?" desiringgod, November 14, 2007, http://www.desiringgod.org/resource -library/ask-pastor-john/how-can-i-discern-the-specific-calling-of-god -on-my-life.

DAY 15: THE PROCESS

1. John 6:5.
2. Often attributed to Mark Twain, quoted in H. Jackson Brown, *P.S. I Love You* (Nashville: Rutledge Hill, 1990), 13.

DAY 21: NATURAL ABILITIES AND SPIRITUAL GIFTS

1. *Chariots of Fire*, directed by Hugh Hudson (UK: Enigma Productions, 1981).
2. Here are a few examples: Tom Rath, Strengths Finder 2.0 (New York: Gallup Press, 2007), https://www.gallupstrengthscenter.com; Lifeway Spiritual Gifts Survey, https:// s3.amazonaws.com/bhpub/edoc/DOC-Spiritual-Gifts -Survey.pdf?AWSAccessKeyId=1FAF154W9TVZ6M3REZ G2&Expires =2105197173 &Signature=Fy8%2FMRHtlDP5kyBPhOVyCCV0xsw%3D; and Spiritual Gifts Test, https://spiritualgiftstest.com.

DAY 24: THREADS OF PLACES

1. Jim Elliot, as quoted by Elisabeth Elliot, *Through Gates of Splendor* (Peabody, MA: Hendrickson Publishers, 1956, 1996), 11.

DAY 28: THREADS OF PASSIONS

1. Eric Metaxas, *Amazing Grace* (New York: HarperCollins, 2007).
2. *Amazing Grace*, directed by Michel Apted (Los Angeles, CA: 20th Century Fox, 2007).

DAY 30: MYSTERY

1. *Merriam-Webster's Dictionary*, s.v. "regenerate," last updated August 14, 2018, https://www.merriam-webster.com/dictionary/regenerate.

DAY 34: SHRINKING BACK

1. Steven Pressfield, *The War of Art* (New York: Black Irish Entertainment, 2002), 12.

DAY 38: FOCUSED AND STEADY

1. Bill Gates, *The Road Ahead* (New York: Penguin, 1996), 316.

DAY 40: THE END OF MUNDANE

1. C. S. Lewis, *The Weight of Glory* (New York: HarperOne, 1949, 2001), 39.

HOW TO FIND GOD

1. Augustine of Hippo, *Saint Augustine's Confessions*, trans. Albert C. Outler (Mineola, NY: Courier Dover Publications: 2002), 103.

ABOUT THE AUTHOR

Jennie Allen is an author, speaker, and the founder and visionary of IF:Gathering. She is a passionate leader following God's call on her life to catalyze a generation to live what they believe. Jennie is the author of *Anything, Nothing to Prove,* and her most recent *New York Times* bestselling book, *Get Out of Your Head.* Her Bible studies include *Stuck, Chase, Restless, Proven,* and *Get Out of Your Head.* Jennie has a master's in biblical studies from Dallas Theological Seminary and lives in Dallas, Texas, with her husband, Zac, and their four children.